Five Nights: A Novel

Anonymous

FIVE NIGHTS

Five Nights

A NOVEL

By
VICTORIA CROSS _(pseud.)_

Cory, Vivian

NEW YORK
MITCHELL KENNERLEY
[c1908]
CB

CONTENTS

FIVE NIGHTS

"The nights have different colours. Some nights are black, the nights of storm: some are electric blue, some are silver, the moon-filled nights: some are red under the hot planet Mars or the fierce harvest moon. Some are white, the white nights of the Arctic winter: but this was a violet night, a hot, mysterious, violet night of Midsummer."

LIFE'S SHOP WINDOW.

INTRODUCTION

As one looks over any period of one's life, it appears behind one as a shining maze of brilliant colour with spots in it here and there of brighter or darker hue. Each spot represents a period of time when our happiness has glowed brighter or waned; sometimes it is a day, more often it is a night. Looking back now, over a stretch of my existence I see many such spots gleaming brightly; they are nights of colour. The history of many of these is too sacred to be written, but there are Five Nights, which, though not the dearest to my memory, have yet stamped themselves and their colour on it for ever. And the record of these five nights is contained in the following pages.

TREVOR LONSDALE.

FIVE NIGHTS

PART ONE
THE GOLD NIGHT

CHAPTER I

THE TAKU INLET

IT was just striking three as I came up the companion-stairs on to the deck of the Cottage City, into the clear topaz light of a June morning in Alaska: light that had not failed through all the night, for in this far northern latitude the sun only just dips beneath the horizon at midnight for an hour, leaving all the earth and sky still bathed in limpid yellow light, gently paling at that mystic time and glowing to its full glory again as the sun rises above the rim.

Our steamer had left the open sea and entered the Taku Inlet, and we were steaming very slowly up it, surrounded on every side by great glittering blocks of ice, flashing in the sunshine as they floated by on the buoyant blue water. How blue it was, the colouring of sea and sky! Both were so vividly blue, the note of each so deep, so intense, one seemed almost intoxicated with colour. I stepped to the vessel's side, then made my way forward and stood there; I, the lover of the East, dazzled by the beauty of the North! The marvellous picture before me was painted in but three colours, blue, gold, and white.

The sides of the inlet were jagged lines of white, the sparkling crystalline whiteness of eternal snow on sharp-pointed, almost lance-like mountain peaks; the water a broad band of blue, the sky above a canopy of blue, and there at the end of the inlet, closing it, like some colossal monster crouched awaiting us, lay the Muir, the huge glacier, a solid wedge of ice, white also, but a transparent white full of blue shadows.

Who shall describe the wonderful air and atmosphere of the North? Its brilliancy, its delicacy, its radiant diamond-like clearness? And the silence, the enchanted stillness of the North? Now as we crept slowly onwards over the vivid water between the flashing icebergs, there was no sound. Complete silence round us, on earth and sea and in the blue vault above, impressive, glittering silence. None of the passengers had broken their sleep to come up to the glory above them, and I stood alone at the forward part of the vessel gliding on through this dream of lustrous blue. Slowly we advanced towards the Muir; very slowly, for these shining bergs carried death with them if they should graze hard against the steamer's side, and, cautiously, steered with infinite pains, the little boat crept on, zigzagging between them. A frail little toy of man, it seemed, to venture here alone; small, black, impertinent atom forcing its way so hardily into this magnificence of colour, this silent splendour, this radiant stillness of the North. Into this very fastness of the most gigantic forces of Nature it had penetrated, and the sapphire sea supported it, the transparent light illumined it, the lance-like mountains looked down upon it, and the glistening bergs forbore to crush it, as if disdaining to harm so fragile a thing.

Very slowly we pushed up the inlet, approaching the shimmering blue-green wall of ice that barred the upper end; seven hundred feet down below the clear surface of the water descends this wall, while three hundred feet of it rise above, forming a glorious shining palisade across the entire width of the inlet. As the sun played on the glittering façade, rays struck out from it as from a reflector, of every shade of green and blue, the deepest hue of emerald mingling with the lightest sapphire, iridescent, sparkling, wonderful. As we crept still nearer, over the living blue of the water, the continual fall of the icebergs from the front wall of the glacier became apparent. At intervals of about five minutes, with a terrific crash like thunder a great wedge of the glittering wall would fall forward into the blue-green depths, and a cloud of snowy spray rise up hundreds of feet into the air. The berg, thus detached, after a few minutes would rise to the surface, glistening, dazzling, and begin its joyous, buoyant voyage downwards to the sea. In all this brilliant setting, with this glory of light around and the triumphal crash of sound like the salute of cannon, amid this joyous movement and in this blaze of colour, amid all that seemed to personify life, we were watching the death of the glacier.

The colossal Muir Glacier, the remains of a world the history of which is lost in the dim twilight none can now penetrate, is dying slowly through a million years. From the mountains, eternally snow-covered, where its huge body, three hundred and fifty miles in extent, has rested through the centuries, it creeps forward slowly towards the sea to meet its doom. Formerly its lip touched the open ocean where now the Taku inlet commences to run inland. But the icy waters, that yet are so much warmer than itself, caressed it with eroding caresses and melted it, and broke bergs from it and rushed inwards, following it till they formed the Taku Inlet, and now the process still goes on, the gigantic body moves forward inch by inch and the green waves break the bergs from its face as the sun invades its structure; and so it lies there, dying slowly through the countless years, glorious, miraculous.

The Captain had promised to approach the face of the glacier as near as was reasonably safe and lie there at anchor for an hour, that the passengers might land at the side of the inlet and those who wished could explore the glacier.

An hour! What was an hour? Those sixty golden minutes would be gone in a flash. Yet it would be an hour of life, of deep emotion, face to face with this monster, strange relic of a forgotten world, stretched on its glorious death-bed.

I was alone still. Not another passenger had yet come up, and I could lean there undisturbed, trying to open my eyes still wider, to expand my heart, to stretch my brain, that I might drink in more of the inimitable grandeur and beauty round me.

The nearer we drew to the glacier the closer packed became the water with the floating bergs; they threatened the ship now on every side, and so slowly did we move we hardly seemed advancing. The bergs flashed and shone as they passed us, rayed through with jewel-like colours, and on one gliding by far from the ship's side I saw two seals at play. For many hundred miles past these seals were the only living things I had seen. The forests on the shore, so thick in the first part of the journey by the Alaskan coast, had long since given way to barren rocks, snow-capped peaks, and ice-filled clefts. No life seemed possible there, the wide distant blue above had shown no bird nor shadow of bird passing. There was no voice of insect nor the least of Nature's children here. Between the thunderous crash of the ice-falls that seemed to shiver the golden air there was intense and solemn stillness.

But the seals played merrily on their floating berg as they passed me, and I watched them long through field-glasses as the joyous, turbulent blue waves carried them far out of my sight towards the open sea.

The clanging of the breakfast bell made me leave my place and go down for a hurried breakfast. I was chilled through, for the early morning air is keen, the pure breath of infinite snowfields, and I took my coffee gratefully amongst the crowd of hungry passengers.

Rough miners some of them, going up to Sitka from the great Treadwell mine at Juneau, traders on their way to Fort Wrangle, and some few explorers. Amongst them were four men our boat had taken on board as we passed the mouth of the Stickeen river. They had started from Canada, lured by the light of the gold that lay under the snows of the Klondike, intending to travel there overland. Losing their way, they had wandered with their pack train for eighteen months in these vast solitudes of ice and snow, groping blindly towards the coast.

Food had failed them, their horses had died by the way from want or fatigue. Faced by starvation, the men had eaten those of their pack animals that had survived, then, finally, when hope had almost left them, they came in sight of the sea.

They were talking of this and their terrible conflict with snow-storm and ice-floe as I joined them, of the plans for making money with which they had started and their failure.

I got away from them all and went back to my place as soon as I could, and spent the rest of the morning as I had begun it, alone at the forward end.

There were very few passengers like myself. Not many people for mere pleasure would take that hazardous voyage along the coast, for it was new country and not a tenth of the sunken rocks and dangerous shoals were yet on any chart. All the way up along that rocky and treacherous shore we had seen the evidences of wreck and disaster everywhere. Above the flats of shimmering water, where the gold or crimson of sunset lay, rose constantly the tops of masts, shadowy and spectral, telling of the sunken hull, the pale corpses beneath those gleaming waves. Ship after ship went down out of those adventurous little coasting vessels that plied up and down the coast trading with the natives, and as we passed these half submerged masts, we often asked ourselves—"Will the Cottage City be more lucky?" She was trading, like all the other boats that go there, with the Alaskan natives, and to go as far north as the Muir was no part of the official programme.

But the fares of the few passengers who really wished

to take all risks and go there was a temptation and overcame the fear of the dreaded Taku Inlet with its monstrous crashing bergs and its possibility of sudden and furious storms. So the little steamer was here, creeping up slowly through this vision of mystic blue towards the glacier, which lay there white, vast, shadowy, mysterious, and my heart beat quicker and quicker as we approached.

I went off in one of the first boats and the moment it touched the pebbly strand of the side of the inlet I jumped out and walked away, eager to be alone to enjoy the glory of it all away from the rasping voices, the worldly talk of my companions, the perpetual "littleness" of ideas that humanity drags with it everywhere.

As I turned from the boat the voices followed me clearly, distinctly, in the exquisite rarefied air.

Thin waves of laughter mingled with them from time to time, growing faint behind me, then the distance closed up between us and I heard no more.

The steamer had landed about thirty passengers and crew, and they seemed immediately lost in these vast expanses. When I had walked a few minutes up the beach from the water's edge, I looked round and was apparently alone. Some few black dots here and there disfiguring the snowy slopes and glittering ice-covered rocks was all that remained of them. In the midst of the vivid blue-green of the inlet behind me, a little wedge of black, lay the steamer, the only reminder that I was one also of these miserable black dots and in an hour I should be collected and taken away as one of them. For this hour, however, I was free and at one with the divine glory about me.

It was just noon. The sky was of a pale and perfect blue, the air still, of miraculous clearness and radiant with the pure light of the North, unshaded, unsoftened by the smallest mist or cloud. The silence was unbroken except for the regular thunder of the falling bergs, that continued with absolute precision at the five-minute interval, and the accompanying splash of the water. I walked on up the strand, having the great glistening wall of the glacier's face somewhat on my left. It was impossible to approach it on land, as the fervid green water lay deep all about its base. It was only at the side of the inlet that little beaches had been formed, and on one of these I stood. The steamer could not get nearer the glacier for fear of the floating bergs, and a small boat could only approach with deadliest peril at the risk of being crushed beneath the falling ice or swamped by the wild division and upheaval of the water that it caused.

But here, on the beach, was a world of enchantment second only in beauty to the glacier itself, for many of the bergs had been stranded there by the playful tides. They stood there now towering up in a thousand different forms, hundreds of feet above one's head, drawing all the light of the sunbeams into their glittering recesses, turning them there into violet, purple, and crimson hues, mauve, saffron, and emerald, blood-red and topaz, and then throwing them out in a million lance-like rays of colour, dazzling and blinding the vision. Like the most wonderful rainbows turned into solid masses they stood there, or like the jewels, rubies, sapphires, and diamonds broken from some giant's crown and scattered recklessly along the strand.

I went up to them and walked beneath an ice arch that glowed rose without as the sun touched it and deepest violet within. Then on, into a cave beyond where the last chamber was coldest white but the outer rim seemed hung with blood-red fire and the middle wall glowed deepest emerald. On, on from one to another, each like a perfect dream of exquisite colour: sunrise and sunset, and all the hues of earth that we ever see were blended together in those glorious bergs.

What a phantasmagoria of colour, what a wonderful vision! Wrapped up in the delight of it, I passed on through some and round others, pursuing my way up the beach, and ascended slowly the rocks, the huge morain at the side of the glacier, while impressively from the inlet came unvaryingly the thunder of the five-minute guns, hastening my steps, dogging them, as it were, with warning of the passing time.

FIVE NIGHTS

After a heavy climb taken too quickly, when I put my foot first on the clear blue-green surface of the glacier, its immensity, its grandeur came home to me. The idea of the huge size of it seems to take the human mind in a curious grip and appal it. Three hundred and fifty square miles of ice stretched round me, white, unbroken, except here and there where gigantic fissures and ravines opened in its surface; ravines where deep blue-green colour glowed in the sides, as if it were the blue-green blood of the glacier. A tiny wind from the north, keen as a knife blade, blew in my face as I stood there, out of the calm blue sky, and seemed to whisper to me of the terrifying nights of storm, of the deadly wind before which all life goes down like a straw, that raged here in the winter. On every side, as far as the eyes could reach, wide white plains of undulating ice and snow, broken here and there by patches of barren rock, that seemed now by some optical delusion, against the glaring white, to be of the brightest mauve and violet tints. Only that; ice and snow and rock for mile upon mile, until the tale of three hundred and fifty is told. No track or trace of bird, no sweet companionship of little furred, four-footed things, no blade of grass or smallest plant or flower, no sound but the roar of the riven ice, the groans of the dying glacier.

I walked on slowly, looking inland towards the white

fields stretching away endlessly into the distance till the blue of the sky seems to come down and mingle with the blue shadows in the snow. Beneath my feet glimmered sometimes the green glass-like surface of smooth ice, at others the thin crisp covering of drifted snow crackled at every step. Sometimes the crevasses were so narrow one could easily walk over them, others yawned widely, many yards across, necessitating a long détour to pass round them.

Looking back from the side of one of them as I walked up it to find the narrowest part, I saw the objectionable black dots had swarmed up on to the edge of the glacier and through the thin, glittering air their voices and laughter at intervals came faintly to me. I sprang over the crevasse and walked on quickly to a point where the fissures grew thick about my feet and the green-blue blood of the glacier glowed in them on every side.

I was looking now down the inlet and was near enough to the face of the glacier to hear, though dulled by distance, the crash of the falling bergs into the foaming water beneath. I could not approach nearer for crevasses hemmed me in; the ice showed itself clear of snow and was so slippery I could hardly stand. One false step now, one small slip and I should disappear down one of these green rents, swallowed up in between those gleaming crystal sides to remain one with the glacier for all time. My idea had been to approach the face of the glacier from the top, but I found this to be as impossible, by reason of the crevasses, as it had been to approach it from the sea on account of the falling bergs.

Sacred, inaccessible, guarded above and below, the great gleaming wall stood there through the centuries, defying the puny curiosity, the feeble efforts of man to even gaze upon it and marvel over it, except from a long distance. I would have given all I had to have been able to advance to the very edge and, kneeling there, look over it down those majestic palisades of white flushed through with green, throwing back to the sun, their destroyer and conqueror, a thousand flashing rays as if in defiance of the slow death being dealt out to them, like one who dies brandishing to the last his sword in the face of his enemy. I longed to look over, down the glimmering wall, to the swelling rush of the green waters as they leapt up rejoicing to receive the colossal diamond-like berg as it crashed down to them, to see them seethe over it and fling their spray high up in the sunshine in mocking revelry; but it was impossible. The fissures in the ice multiplied themselves as one neared the edge and now were spread round my feet in a perfect network, like the meshes of a snare. It was impossible to go forward, and I was unwilling to go back. I stood motionless on a little tongue of polished ice between two blue-green chasms, so deep that they seemed riven down to the very heart of the glacier; stood there, drinking in the keen gold air and the beauty of the blue arch above, of the boundless spaces of glittering white round me, of the narrow green inlet so far below from which echoed the reverberating roar of the falling ice.

I was debating with myself, should I stay here alone for a time, letting the steamer go, after having stored some provisions for me on the shore, and call again for me a few weeks later, in any case before the short summer of these northern latitudes was over, and winter closed the inlet?

To stay here alone, the one single human being, in a thousand miles of space, and not only the one human being, but the one *life*, with no companionship of animal, bird, or insect, that would be an experience of solitude indeed!

The idea attracted me; all day and all night to hear nothing but that thunderous roar, and see nothing but the shining sea, the gleaming ice-fields, and the glittering bergs, to be alone with Nature, to see her, as it were, intimately in her awful beauty, with breast and brow unveiled—and, perhaps, have death as one's reward!

There was fascination in the thought.

What ideas would come to one as one watched the

little steamer, the only link that held one still bound to the world of men, weigh anchor and steam slowly down the green inlet, departing and leaving one behind it, as one watched it growing smaller, dwindling ever, till it was a mere speck, and then saw it vanish, leaving the green riband of water unbroken save for the passing bergs? How one would realise solitude when the boat had absolutely disappeared, and how that solitude would thrill through and through one's blood as the long light night rolled by and dawn and day succeeded with their unvarying march of silent glittering hours!

And if death came on the wings of a storm such as rises suddenly in these regions and piled high the snow over the camp, freezing the inmate, or if it came by slow starvation, the steamer having been lost on that dangerous rocky coast and none other having come in time, how would death seem to one here, already so far removed from men and all desire and lust of the world, here, where already all earthly things had almost ceased to be and one's spirit had merged into the Infinite?

Death would seem to one in different guise from when he comes to us in the midst of the delights of the world, with the baubles of life around us, or in the stress of the battle-field in the moment of victory, surrounded by our comrades.

Death here would come but as the crown, the climax

to the solitude, the detachment, the isolation, would seem but as the laying down the head on the breast of Nature, becoming one with her immensity, her grandeur.

For some minutes I was keenly tempted to stay, the idea held my mind and fascinated it, but with the vision of death came the recoil from it born from the remembrance of my art. The same recoil that had saved me many times before, for youth is usually greatly inclined to suicide, either directly or indirectly in the dangers it courts. But in an artist this is strangely balanced by his love for his work. When he has ceased to wish for life or heed it for himself he still feels instinctive revolt against extinguishing that diviner spark than life itself, his genius, lent him from the celestial fire.

The thought of my work dispelled the enchanted dream into which I had fallen. Instinctively I turned and very slowly began to retrace my steps amongst the yawning pitfalls. As I did so I heard a hoarse hoot from the steamer lying below, to tell me it was about to leave, another and another resounded dully from it, warning me to hasten my return.

I made my way back to the shore where the boat and the impatient sailors awaited me. I took my seat in it, turning my eyes to the glistening, glimmering white palisade rising over the sapphire sea.

When we had reached the steamer and its head was turned round I stood at the stern and watched that palisade for long, as it receded and receded. At last the blue distance swallowed it up. I could see no more than a silvery line dividing the blues of meeting sea and sky. Then I went down to my cabin and locked the door and lay down on my berth in the quiet, trying to live over again that one hour of close contact with the beauty of the North.

After dinner that night I wrote a long letter to my cousin Viola about the beauty of the Muir. She would understand, I knew. What I thought she would feel, for our brains were cast in the same mould. The letter finished, it was still too early to go to bed; so I picked up a curious book called "Life's Shop Window" which I had been reading the previous night, and read this passage which had struck me before, over again:

"So, as we look into our future, we see ourselves beloved and wealthy; victorious, famous, and free to wander through the sweetest paths of the world, passing through a thousand scenes, sometimes loving, sometimes warring, tasting and drinking of everything sweet and stimulating, knowing all things, enjoying all in turn; but this is the life of a God, not a man. And it is perhaps the God in us which so savagely demands the life of a God.

"But it is not granted to us."

Yet this was the life I was trying to lead, and to some extent I succeeded. Change, change, it is the life of life, perhaps especially to the artist.

And I was an artist now, thanks to the decision of the Royal Academy last year to accept the worst picture I had submitted to them for four years. Ever since my fingers could clasp round anything at all they had loved to hold a brush; for years in my teens I had studied painting under the best teachers of technique in Italy. For two or three years I had done really good work, with the divine afflatus thrilling through every vein. And last year I had painted rather a commonplace picture and it had been hung on the line in the Academy, and so my friends all said I really was an artist now, and I modestly accepted the style and title, with outward diffidence.

How little any of them guessed, as they congratulated me, of the wild rapture of feeling, of intense gratitude with which I had listened to the Divine whisper that had come to my ears as a boy of seventeen sitting in a small bare bedroom, on the floor with the sheet of paper before me on which I had drawn a woman's head. As I looked at it, I knew suddenly my power, and the Voice that is above all others said within me: "*I* have made you an artist. None can undo or dispute MY work."

From that moment I cared for neither praise nor

blame. The opinion of men affected me not at all. My gift was mine, and I knew it. I held it straight from the Divine hands. I had the Divine promise with me for as long as I should live on this earth.

And I was filled with a boundless delight in life and my own powers.

When I showed my original pictures all painted under inspiration to my father, he carefully put on his pince-nez and studied them very closely. After that he said he must reserve his judgment. When they went to the Academy and were promptly refused, he drew a long face and said I had better have gone into the Indian Civil Service as he wished. Subsequently, when I had sold them all, and not one for less than a thousand guineas, he began to enter upon a placid state of contentment with me which induced him to say to other captious relations—"Let the boy alone, he will be an artist some day." At which I used to laugh inwardly and go away to my studio to listen to the Divine voice dictating fresh pictures to me. For five years in Italy I had studied closely and worked unremittingly, keeping myself for my art alone and existing only in it. My teachers had called me industrious. Another phrase which always must make an artist laugh when applied to his art.

To those who know the wild pleasure, the almost mad joy of exercising a really natural gift, it sounds as funny as to talk of a drunkard industriously getting drunk.

However, this by the way. The world is the world, and artists are artists; the artist may understand the world, but the world can never understand the artist.

I was happy, life passed like a golden dream till I was twenty-two, and my father was satisfied that I was an "industrious" student.

From twenty-two till now, when I was twenty-eight, life had opened out into fuller colour still. My art remained the life of the soul, of all that was best in me, but the brain and the senses had come forward, demanding their share of recognition, too, and out of the many coloured strands of which we can weave our web of life, I had chosen that which gleams the next brightest to art, the strand of passion, and woven much with that.

I had travelled, passing from country to country, city to city, finding love and inspiration everywhere, for the world is full of both for those who desire and look for them, and now I had come on this coasting trip along the shores of Alaska in the same spirit, looking for pictures in the golden atmosphere, for joy in the golden days and nights.

My sketch-book was full of ideas and jottings, and I looked forward much to the landing at Sitka where I hoped to find new and good material. The hopeless

ugliness of the Alaskan natives had so far appalled me.
An artist chiefly of the face and figure, as I was, could
not hope to find a model amongst them. As our
steamer had come up the coast I had looked in vain
for even a decent-sized woman or child amongst them.
They seem a race without a single beauty, possessing
neither stature, nor colour, nor length of hair, nor
even plump shapeliness. Undersized, leather-skinned,
small-eyed, thin, and wizened, they never seem to be
young. They seem to start middle-aged and go on
growing older.

No, I had really had no luck at present on my Alaskan
tour, but I was naturally sanguine and hoped still
something from Sitka.

Most capitals give you something if you visit them,
and Sitka was the capital of Alaska.

As I lay in my berth that night, made wakeful by the
bright light, I was thinking over past incidents in my
life and all the Minnies and Marys that had been
connected with them. They seemed all to have been
Mary or Minnie with Marias in Italy and France.
I fell asleep at last, hoping whatever Fate had in store
for me at Sitka, it wouldn't be a Mary or a Minnie,
but some new name embodying a new idea.

CHAPTER II

THE TEA-SHOP

WHEN we landed at Sitka I went ashore with a fellow-passenger. He was a clever man, and had made trips up there already for the sake of taking photographs of the people and the scenery; he knew Sitka well and came up to me just before we arrived there with the remark:

"If you come with me I'll take you to have tea with the prettiest girl you've ever seen."

This certainly seemed an invitation to accept, and I did so on the spot.

"She really is," he continued, observing my sceptically raised eyebrows, "wonderfully pretty. She keeps a tea-shop and she is Chinese." With that he bolted into his own cabin, which was next mine, and as I heard him laughing, I concluded he was joking and thought no more about it. However, as the ship glided up over flat sheets of golden water to the landing-stage, he joined me again, and together we stood looking up the principal street of Sitka which runs down to meet the little quay.

It was just four in the afternoon, and everything was vivid living gold, as the floods of yellow sunshine filled all the shining air. The green copper dome of the church alone stood out a soft spot of delicate colour in the dazzling burnished haze.

30

At the sides of the street sat and crouched the small squat figures of the Alaskan Indians, each with a mat before it, on which the owner had set out his little store of wares—bottles of various-coloured sands, reindeer slippers beautifully embroidered in blue beads, carved walrus teeth.

We stepped on the shore and the Indians looked up at us with quaint brown questioning eyes, like their own seals.

They did not ask you to buy, but watched you silently.

"Come along," said my friend, "we'll go up and get tea before there's a crowd."

After about five minutes' walk, while I was gazing about interested in this quaint little capital, my companion suddenly exclaimed:

"In here," and turned through an opening at the corner of a square enclosure on our right hand. I followed, and saw we had entered a little square court or compound, similar to those with which the poorer classes in any Eastern community surround their huts.

The floor was dried and hardened mud, the walls about seven feet high, and numerous small tables laid for tea stood round them.

My companion did not pause here, however, but went straight through in at the low house door, and we found ourselves in a very small, dark passage, hung with red and with red cloths dangling from the ceiling, that swept our heads as we came in.

It seemed quite dark inside, coming from the fierce gold light of the streets, but there was a dim little lamp in Eastern glass of many colours swinging somewhere at the farther end, and we found our way down to a low door in the side of the passage. This brought us into a small square room which gave the impression of being sunk below the level of the street. There were diminutive windows in the outer wall, but they were close to the low ceiling and though the glorious light from without tried hard to come in, it was successfully obstructed by little rush blinds of red and green. The rushes were placed vertically side by side and fastened together with string and painted in bright tints. The breeze from the sea came through them and sang a low song of its own. The walls were hung with red stuff curtains, over which ramped wonderful Chinese dragons in green; the floor was spread with something soft, on which the feet made no sound; in the corners of the room stood some little tables.

To the farthest of these, under the rush-covered windows, we made our way and sat down on some very ordinary American chairs, a hideous note in the quaint surrounding, introduced as a concession, no doubt, to Western taste.

"I rather like this, Morley," I said as I took my seat and looked round.

"Thought you would," he returned, and pressed his hand on a tiny bronze figure standing on the table. At the touch of his finger the head of the figure disappeared between its shoulders, and then sprung up again, producing a harsh clanging sound of a gong.

Hardly a moment later the red curtains that hung over the doorway parted, and a figure came into the room.

Such a sweet figure, the very spirit of poetic girlhood seemed incarnate before us.

In appearance she was a Chinese maiden of seventeen or eighteen years; seventeen or eighteen according to our standard of looks, doubtless she was in reality younger.

The face was wonderfully beautiful, a very rounded oval and of the most perfect creamy tint, the nose, straight and fine, was rather long, the upper lip short, and the mouth very small, soft, and full-lipped. The eyes inclined a little to the Chinese shape, but were large, wide, and well-opened and brimming to the lids with extraordinary light and fire; delicately narrow black eyebrows arched above on the low satiny forehead, from which was brushed upwards a mass of shining black hair piled on the top of the small head and apparently secured there by two weighty gold pins thrust through from side to side.

The last touch of beauty, if any were needed, was added by the earrings of turquoise-blue stone that swung against the ivory-tinted softness of the full young throat.

Those blue stones against the creamy neck! For years afterwards how I could see them again in the darkness that lies behind closed lids! How often I was back in the crimson darkness of the tiny chamber with the sea song of the Alaskan waves coming through the painted rushes above my head!

She was very simply dressed, yet so fitly to her own beauty.

A straight pale blue jacket covered her shoulders and opened on the breast over a white muslin vest. Her skirts hung like the full trousers of Persian women, and were a deep yellow in colour. Her feet were bare, and shone white on the red floor.

"How do you do, Suzee?" said Morley.

"How do you do, Mister Morlee," returned the girl lightly, smiling and showing pretty little teeth as she did so.

"You two gentlemen want some tea? Very good. I make it."

She glided to the curtains and disappeared as rapidly and noiselessly as she had entered.

I turned to Morley with enthusiasm.

"She's lovely, perfect."

"Isn't she just? I knew you'd say so. But she's married, old man, so don't you think you can go playing any tricks with her."

"Married?" I gasped incredulously, "that child? Impossible! You're joking."

"I'm not, 'pon my honour. She has a great roaring brute of a baby, too."

"How horrible!" I exclaimed. "Yes, horrible. You've spoiled it all. It seems a sacrilege."

"Fiddlesticks," returned my practical friend. "That's the sort that does these things, isn't it? Would you expect her to turn into an old maid?"

"No, but so young!" I faltered. In reality it was a shock to me. To have such an exquisite sight float before one for a moment, and then to be roughly dragged down to earth from the exaltation it had caused, hurt and bruised me.

The next moment she was back again, bearing a tray in her hands which she set on our table, and deftly arranged the steaming tea-pot and tiny cups before us.

As she bent near us over the little table a strange sensation of delight came over me, a faint scent of roses reached me from the little buds behind her ear. The blue stones in the long gold earrings swung against her neck of cream as she set out the tea things.

"How is your boy, Suzee?" asked Morley with a tone of mischief in his voice.

"He is very well, thank you, Mister Morlee."

"I should like to see him. Will you bring him in?" he continued, commencing to pour out the tea.

"Yes; he is asleep now, but I will wake him up," she returned nonchalantly, and, in spite of a protestation from me, she went out to do so.

After a minute we heard loud screams from across the passage and presently Suzee reappeared dragging (I can use no other phrase) in her arms an enormous baby. Its face was red, and it was roaring lustily. The girl-mother did not seem disturbed in the least by its cries, but staggered slowly over to us, clasping the child awkwardly round the waist and holding it flat against her own body.

It seemed very large, out of all proportion to the small and exquisitely dainty mother. She was short and small, and the child really, as I looked at it, seemed to be quite half the length of her own body.

"What a big boy he is," remarked Morley.

"Yes, isn't he?" said the mother proudly.

The baby roared its loudest, tears streamed down its scarlet face, and it dug its clenched knuckles furiously into its eyes.

"Surely it's in pain," I suggested.

"Oh, he always cries when he is woken up," returned the mother tranquilly. She did not seem to take the least notice of the child's bellowing. She might have been deaf for all the effect it had upon her. She stood there placidly holding it, though it seemed very heavy for her, while the child screamed itself purple. She began a conversation with Morley just precisely as if the child were non-existent.

I never saw such a picture, and it struck me suddenly I should like to paint it, just as it was there, and call the thing "Maternity."

But no. What would be the good? No one, certainly not the British public, would ever believe its truth.

They would think it a joke, and a grotesque one at that. "Beauty and the Beast" would do for a name, I mused, or "Fact and Fancy."

Nothing could be more delicately soul-absorbingly beautiful than the mother; nothing so brutally hideous as the child.

Suzee had sat down on the floor now, and the baby, still roaring, had rolled on to its face on the ground beside her. Still she took not the smallest notice of it; she laid one shapely hand on the small of its back, as if to make sure it was there, and continued her conversation tranquilly with Morley. How she could hear what he said I could not tell. I could hear nothing but the appalling row the child made.

"Do take it away," I said after a few moments more, in an interval of yells, during which the baby rolled,

apparently in the last stages of suffocation, on the floor.
"I can't stand that noise."

"Ah!" said Suzee meditatively, lifting her glorious
almond eyes to mine, "you do not like my boy-baby?"

"I do not like the noise he makes," I said evasively,
"and I don't think he can be well, either."

"Oh yes, he is quite well," she returned composedly;
"but I will take him away."

So saying, she began to haul at the loose things about
the child's waist, as a tired gardener hauls at a sack of
potatoes prior to lifting it up.

I thought really she would get the child into her
arms head downwards, so carelessly did she seem to
manage it, and as she rose and carried it to the door
it seemed as if the awkward weight of it must strain her
own slight body.

When the curtain closed behind her and the screams
got faint in the distance as the unhappy child was hauled
to a back room, I drew a breath of relief and began to
drink my tea, which really hitherto I had been too
nervous to do. Morley chuckled and remarked:

"Good for you to be disillusioned."

"I'm not in the least, with *her*. She is a divine
piece of physical beauty. I wish I could get her on my
canvas."

"You won't be able to; that old curmudgeon of a
husband of hers will see to that."

"I should think he has the devil of a temper, judging by his offspring," I answered. "She looks sweet enough."

Morley nodded, and we finished our tea in silence. Suzee came back presently with cigarettes for us and sat down on the floor herself, rolling one up between supple fingers. She had an air of extraordinary unruffled placidity. The dragging about of the child had not disturbed her dress nor heated her face. In cool, tranquil, placid beauty she sat and rolled cigarettes while the child's cries dimly echoed in the distance.

"Where's the boss, Suzee?" questioned Morley presently.

"He has gone down to Fort Wrangle for two days," she returned, and my spirits leapt up at her words. Her husband away for two days! Perhaps there was a chance for a picture. . . .

My eyes swept over her seated on the floor in front of us. What exquisite supple lines! What sweet little dainty curves showed beneath the blue silk jacket and sleeve! What a glory of light and passionate expression in the liquid dark eyes when she raised them to us!

After a few minutes Morley got up, and I saw him laying down on the table the money for our tea. I added my share, and Morley remarked,

"We'd better go and walk about before dinner, hadn't we? You'd like a look round?"

I was gazing at Suzee.

"Do you have any time to yourself?" I asked her. "Later in the evening perhaps when you could come for a walk with me."

Suzee looked up. There was surprise in those wonderful eyes, but I thought I saw pleasure too.

"At six," she said. "I close the restaurant for a short time, but I don't walk, I smoke and go to sleep. But I will come with you if it is not too far," she added as an after-thought.

Morley gave a whistle, indicative of surprise and disapproval, but I answered composedly.

"Very well, I shall come here at six; so don't be asleep and fail to let me in!"

Suzee laughed and shook her head, and we picked up our hats and went out of the little room into the passage. In the outer court, as we passed through, we saw most of the tables occupied, and an elderly woman serving.

"We had the best of it," I remarked.

"Yes, rather. But you are going ahead with that girl. Do be careful or you'll have the old terror of a husband down on you."

"You introduced me," I returned laughing. "You have all the responsibility."

"You know dinner's at six on this unearthly boat. Aren't you going to get any dinner to-night?"

"I'm not very particular about it. I shall pick up something. I thought six when all the men would be back on board would be her free time."

"But what are you going to do with her?"

"Get her to pose for me, if she will."

"Anything else?"

"One never knows in life," I answered smiling.

Morley regarded me thoughtfully.

"You artists do manage to have a good time."

"You could have just the same if you chose," I said.

"No, I don't think I could somehow," he answered slowly. "I am not so devilishly good-looking as you are, for one thing."

"Oh, I don't know," I replied; "and does that make much difference with women, do you think? Isn't it rather a passionate responsiveness, a go-ahead-ness, that they like?"

"Yes, I think it is, but then that's it, you've got that. I don't think I have. I don't seem to want the things, to see anything in them, as you do."

I laughed outright. We were walking slowly down one of the gold, light-filled streets towards the church now, and everything about us seemed vibrating in the dazzling heat.

"If you don't want them I should think it's all right." I said.

"No, it isn't," returned my companion gravely. "You want a thing very much and you get it, and have no end of fun. I don't want it and don't get it, and don't have the fun. So it makes life very dull."

"Well, I *am* very jolly," I admitted contentedly. "I think really, artists—people with the artist's brain —do enjoy everything tremendously. They have such a much wider field of desires, as you say; and fewer limitations. They 'weave the web Desire,' as Swinburne says, 'to snare the bird Delight.'"

"They get into a mess sometimes," said Morley sulkily; "as you will with that girl if you don't look out. Here we are at the church. There's a very fine picture inside; you'd like to see it, I expect."

We turned into the church and rested on the chairs for a few minutes, enjoying the cool dark interior.

At six o'clock exactly I was in the little mud-yard again, before the tea-shop; having sent Morley off to his dinner on board. I felt elated: all my pulses were beating merrily. I was keenly alive. Morley was right in what he said. An artist is Nature's pet, and she has mixed all his blood with joy. Natural, instinctive joy, swamped occasionally by melancholy, but always there surging up anew. Joy in himself— joy in his powers—joy in life.

I knocked as arranged, and Suzee herself let me in. She had been burning spice, apparently, before one of the idols that stood in each corner of the tea-shop; for the whole place smelt of it.

"What have you been doing?" I said. "Holding service here?"

"Only burning spice-spills to chase away the evil spirits," replied Suzee.

"Are there any here?" I inquired.

"They always come in with the white foreign devils," she returned with engaging frankness.

I laughed.

"Well, Suzee, you are unkind," I expostulated. "Is that how you think of me?"

She looked up with a calm smile.

"The devil is always welcomed by a woman," she answered sweetly—her eyes were black lakes with fire moving in their depths—"that is one of our proverbs. It is quite true."

The lips curled and the creamy satin of the cheeks dimpled and the blue earrings shook against her neck.

"What lovely earrings," I said, smiling down upon her, and put up my hand gently to touch one. She did not draw back nor seem to resent my action.

"You think them pretty? I have others upstairs. Will you come up and see my jewellery?"

I assented with the greatest willingness, and we went on down the passage and then up the narrow, steep flight of stairs at the end.

43

"Don't wake up your child," I said in sudden horror, as we reached the small square landing above of slender rickety uncovered boards.

"Oh, he never wakes till one pulls him up," she answered tranquilly, and led the way into a little chamber. Did she sleep here? I wondered. There was no bed, but a loose heap of red rugs in one corner. The windows were mere narrow horizontal slits close to the ceiling. In the centre, blocking up all the space, stood a high narrow chest. It looked very old, of blackened wood and antique shape. I had never seen such a thing. On the top of this, which nearly came to her chin, she eagerly spread out heaps of little paper parcels she took from one of the drawers.

"Have you any earrings just like those you are wearing?" I asked her. If she had, I would buy them if I could for my cousin Viola, I thought. Viola was excessively fair, and those blue stones would be enchanting against her blonde hair.

"You want to buy them?" she said quickly. "I have a pair here just like, only green. Buy those."

"No," I said. "It is the colour I like. Do you want to sell these blue ones you are wearing?"

"No," she said quickly; "not these," and ran to a small mirror on the wall and looked in hastily, fearfully, as if she thought that by wishing for them I could charm them away from her out of her very ears.

That she appreciated so well the effect of the colour harmony between the blue stones and her own cream-hued skin, and the value of it in setting off her beauty, pleased me. It seemed to augur well for her artistic sense.

"May I sit down here?" I asked her, going to the pile of scarlet rugs and cushions in the corner.

"Oh yes, Meester Treevor, sit down," and she came hastily forward to rearrange them for me with Oriental politeness. I sat down, drawing up my legs as I best could, and pointed to a place beside me.

"Come and sit down, Suzee," I said; "I have something to show you now."

She came and sat beside me, but not very close, with her knees raised and her smooth lissom little hands clasped round them. Her almond eyes grew almost round with curiosity. I had brought with me a small portfolio of some of my sketches with the object of introducing the subject of her posing for me. I opened it and drew out the topmost sketch. It was the figure of a young Italian girl lying on a green bank beneath some vines. She was not wholly undraped, but most of her attire was on the bank beside her, and the rest was of a transparent gauzy nature suited to the heat suggested in the sunlit picture.

The moment Suzee's eyes fell upon it she gave a shriek of dismay and covered her face with her hands.

Over any portion I could still see of it spread the Eastern's equivalent of a blush: a sort of dull heavy red that seems to thicken the tissues.

"What is the matter?" I asked, surveying her in surprise. There was nothing in the picture which would cause the least embarrassment to any English girl.

"Oh, Treevor, it is dreadful to look at things like that," she exclaimed, moving her fingers before her face and looking at me with one eye through them. Then she made some rapid passes over her head, as if to ward off the evil spirits I had conjured up.

I laughed.

"You may think so, Suzee," "I said; but in our country, and many others, these 'things,' as you call them, are not only very much looked at, but also admired, and bought and sold for great sums. What do you see so very bad in it?"

Suzee ventured to peer through her fingers with both eyes at the fearful object.

"Dreadful!" she exclaimed again, quickly shutting her fingers. "It is a very bad woman, is it not?"

"No," I said, somewhat nettled; "certainly not. This was quite a respectable girl. I have quantities of these portraits and sketches. Look here," and I opened the portfolio and spread out several pictures on the rug.

Suzee drew herself together, tightly pursed up her

lips, and looked down at them with alarm,—as if I had let loose a number of snakes.

"They are very, very wicked things," she said, primly as a dissenting minister's wife; and lowered her eyelids till the lashes lay like black silk on the cheeks.

I gathered the offending sketches together and pushed them back under cover.

"I wanted you to pose for me," I said, "that I might have your picture, too; but I expect you won't do so for me?"

"I! I!" said Suzee, with virtuous indignation, "be put on paper like that? I would die first." Her face had thickened all over as the blood went into it. Her eyes looked stormy, alluring.

I leant towards her suddenly as we sat side by side, put my arms round her waist, drew her to me, and pressed my lips on the ridiculous little screwed-up mouth, with a sudden access of passion that left her breathless.

"You are a horrid little humbug, and goose, and prude," I said, laughing, as I released her. "What do you think of letting me kiss you like that, then? Is that wrong?"

Suzee sighed heavily, swaying her pliable body only a very little way from me.

"It may be—a little " she admitted; "but it's not like the pictures."

"Oh! It's not so bad—not so wicked?" I asked mockingly.

"Oh no, not nearly," she returned decisively.

"Well," I answered, "many people would think it much worse. Those girls who have let me draw them would not let me kiss them—some of them," I added. "So, you see, it's a matter of opinion and idea. Now, will you say why the picture is so much worse than a kiss?"

"A kiss," murmured Suzee, "is just between two people. It is done, and no one knows. It is gone." She spread out her hands and waved them in the air with an expressive gesture. "Those things remain a monument of shame for ever and ever."

I laughed. I was beginning to see there was not much chance of a picture, but other prospects seemed fair. In life one must always take exactly what it offers, and neither refuse its goods nor ask for more, either in addition or exchange. Sitka would give me something, but perhaps not a picture as I had hoped.

I looked at her in silence for some seconds, musing on her curious beauty.

"I shall call you 'Sitkar-i-buccheesh,'" I said after a minute.

Suzee looked frightened and made a rapid pass over her head.

"What is that?" she asked. "It sounds a devil's name."

48

"It only means the gift of Sitka," I answered. "This city has given you to me, has it not? or it will," I added in a lower tone.

I put my arm round her again, and she leant towards me as a flower swayed by the breeze, her head drooped and rested against my shoulder.

"If it were the name of a devil," I said laughing, "it would suit you. I believe you are an awful little devil."

"All women are devils," returned Suzee placidly.

I did not answer, but Viola's face swam suddenly before my vision—a face all white and gold and rose and with eyes of celestial blue.

"What would your husband say to all this?" I asked jestingly.

"He will never know. I tell him quite different. He believes everything I say."

Involuntarily I felt a little chill of disgust pass through me. Deceit of any kind specially repels me, and deceit towards some one trusting, confident, is the worst of all.

Perhaps she read my thoughts instinctively, for she said next, in a pleading note, to enlist my sympathies:

"He is very, very cruel, he beats me all the time."

I looked down at her as she lay in the cradle of my arm, a little sceptical.

From what I knew of the Chinese character it did not seem at all likely that Hop Lee did beat his wife; more-

over, the delicate, fragile, untouched beauty of the girl
did not allow one to imagine she had suffered, or could
suffer much violence.

Again she seemed to feel my doubt of her, for she
pushed up suddenly her sleeve with some trouble from
one velvet-skinned arm and pushed it up before my
eyes. There was a deep dull crimson mark upon it the
size of a half-crown.

"Unbeliever! Look at this bruise."

I looked at it, then at her steadily.

"Suzee, did your husband make that bruise?"

"Yes. He pinched me so hard in a rage with me,"
she said a little sulkily.

"Give me your arm," I said.

She held it out reluctantly. I looked at the bruise,
then I rolled the sleeve back a little farther, and in it
found a heavy gold bangle with a boss on one side
corresponding with the size of the mark on the flesh.

"I think it is the gold bracelet your kind old husband gave you that you have pressed into the flesh,"
I said, "that has marked it. That is about what his
cruelty to you amounts to." I dropped her arm contemptuously, and rose suddenly.

She had succeeded in dispelling for the moment the
charm of her beauty. Her prudery, her deceit, her
lies made up to me a peculiarly obnoxious mixture.

She sprang up, too, as I rose and threw herself on her

knees, clasping her arms round mine so that I could not move.

"Oh, Treevor, I do love you so much. You are my real master, not he. A woman loves a man who conquers her, but not by buying her. But because he is better and stronger than she. Because he has great muscles, as you have, and could kill her, and because she can't deceive him, because he sees all her lies, as you do. Yes, Treevor, I love you now very much indeed. Come here again, kiss me again."

But somehow her pleading did not move me. The moment when I had been drawn to her had gone by, swallowed up in a feeling of disgust.

. I stooped down and unlocked her hands and put her back among her cushions.

"Good-bye, Suzee, for to-day," I said. "To-morrow I will come and take you for a walk. You must let me go now. I do not want to stay any longer."

She looked at me in silence, but did not offer to move from where I had put her.

I gathered up my portfolio and left the room, went down the stairs and through the passage and court-yard to the sun-filled street.

I went on slowly, and after a time found myself close to the church again. I went in, for the interior interested me, and found service was being held. A Russian priest, wholly in white clothing, stood before the altar, the cross light from the aisle windows falling on the long twist of fair hair that lay upon his shoulders. The whole air was full of incense that rose in white clouds to the domed roof. I sat down near the door and listened while the priest intoned a Latin hymn. The figure of the young priest at the altar attracted me. I thought I should like a sketch of it; but I hesitated to take one of him in the church, even surreptitiously, so I fixed the picture of him as he stood there on my eyes as far as I could, and then, in a convenient pause of the service, quietly slipped outside.

Near the church was a great outcrop of rock surmounted by a weather-beaten tree. In the shade thrown by these I got out a sheet of loose paper and made a sketch of the fair, long-haired priest, with the quaint frame building of the church, its green copper dome and bell tower and double gold crosses behind him.

After I had been there some time I was suddenly surprised by Morley.

"Hullo!" he exclaimed. "You here? Why, I thought you would be in the arms of the fair Suzee by this time."

"So I might have been," I answered, looking up from the sketch, "but I got put off somehow, so I left her and went to church instead!"

Morley burst out laughing.

"You *are* the funniest fellow," he exclaimed, taking his seat beside me on the ground and clasping his hands round his knees. "So Suzee has offended you, has she? Do you know, I think that's where we ordinary people get ahead of fellows like you. You are too sensitive. We're not so particular. When I'm stuck on Mary Ann it doesn't matter to me what she says or does. It doesn't interfere with my happiness."

I went on painting in silence.

"Funny those chaps look with their long hair, don't they?" he remarked after a moment, as I painted the light on the priest's long curl.

"Very picturesque, don't you think?" I said.

"No, I don't," returned the Briton stoutly. "I think it's beastly."

I laughed this time, and having completed the portrait, slipped it into my portfolio and prepared to put away my paints.

"Don't you want any dinner?" asked Morley. "You must be hungry."

"Well, I hadn't thought of it," I answered. "But, now you mention it, perhaps I am. Do you know of any place where one can get anything?"

"There's one place at the end of the town where you can have soup and bread," replied Morley, and we started off to find it.

53

Later on, towards ten o'clock, when we were leaving the little, frame, sailors' restaurant, I looked up to the western sky and saw that strange colour in it of the Alaskan sunset that I have never found in any other sky, a bright magenta, or deep heather pink, a crude colour rather like an aniline dye, but brilliant and arresting in the clean, clear gold of the heavens.

Great ribs and bars and long flat lines of it lay all across the West. No other cloud, no other colour appeared anywhere in the sky. It was painted in those two tints alone; the brightest magenta conceivable and living gold.

Walking back slowly to the ship, I gazed at it with interest. No other sky that I could recall ever shows this tone of colour. Pink, scarlet, rose, and all the shades of blood or flame-colour are familiar in every sunset, but this curious tint seemed to belong to Alaska alone.

I watched it glow and deepen, then fade, and softly disappear as the sun dipped below the horizon.

CHAPTER III

IN THE WOOD

THE next evening, after dinner, I left the ship and made my way to Suzee's place to take her for the promised walk.

It was just seven when I stepped ashore, and light of the purest, most exquisite gold lay over everything. The air had that special quality of Alaska which I have never met anywhere else, an extreme humidity; it hung upon the cheek as a mist hangs, only it was clear as crystal, brilliant as a yellow diamond.

There was no wind, not a breath ruffled the stillness nor stirred the motionless blue water.

The exquisite chain of islands off the mainland was mirrored in the still, shining depths, and lifted their delicate outlines clothed with fir and larch, soft as half-forgotten dreams, against the transparent blue of the sky. Sitka was placid and restful, the streets quiet and empty as I walked along in the sunny silence.

Suzee was at the door waiting for me. She had dressed herself differently, entirely in yellow. The yellow silk of the little square jacket contrasted well with her midnight hair, and the only dash of other colour in the picture she presented was the blue stone in her earrings.

"Good evening, Treevor," she said, smiling up at

me. And I bent down and pressed my lips to those little, soft, curved ones she put up for me.

We started out at once. Suzee told me we were going for a long way to see the wood, and had the important air of a person going on a lengthy expedition. She had brought a Japanese sunshade with her which she put up, and certainly the hot light falling through the rice-paper had a wonderfully beautiful effect on her creamy skin and soft yellow silk clothing. She walked easily, only with rather short steps. As she was of the lower class, there had been no question of the "golden lilies" or distortion of the feet for her, and they were small and prettily shaped, bare, save for a sort of sandal, or as the Indians call them, "guaraches," bound under the sole.

We passed up the main street and soon after turned into a narrow winding road that leads along the coast, Sitka being on a promontory, with a beautiful azure bay running inland behind it.

Our path ran sometimes inland, through portions of wood, part of that great impenetrable primeval forest that at one time completely covered the whole of Sitka, sometimes quite on the edge of the water. Here there were rocks and boulders, and little coves of white sand and stretches of miniature beaches, with the lip of the bay resting on them.

Infinitesimal waves broke on the sunny white sand

56

with a low musical tinkle, across the bay one could
see the delicate chain of islands rising with their feath-
ery trees into the blue, warding off the breakers and
the storms of the open sea beyond. In here, the
peaceful water murmured to itself and repeated tales
of the beginning of the world, of the first gold dawn
that broke upon the earth, and of later days, when the
sombre black forests came to the water's edge and none
knew them but the great black bear, and when the
seals played joyously, undisturbed, in the fog-banks
off the islands. I was in the mood to appreciate
deeply the beauty of the scene, and all the objects
round seemed to speak to me of their inner meaning,
but my companion was not at all moved by, nor interested in her surroundings. She helped to make the
picture more strange and lovely as she sat by me on a
rock, with her shining clothes and brilliant face under
the gay sunshade, but mentally she jarred on me by
her complete indifference to any influence of the scene.
I almost wished I were alone here, to sit upon this tremendous shore and dream.

"You are dull, Treevor," she exclaimed pettishly.
"You really are."

I had kissed her twice in the last ten minutes, but
she hated my eyes to wander for a moment from her
face to the sea. She hated the least reference apparently to the landscape. As long as I was talking to

her and about her, admiring her dress or her hair, she was satisfied.

"Come along," she said impatiently; "let us go on to the wood, leave off looking at that stupid sea."

I rose reluctantly and we followed the road which turned inland again. The wood was a world of grey shadows. As we entered by a narrow trail leading from the road, the golden day outside was soon closed from us by the thick veils of hanging creeper and parasitical plants of all sorts that entwined round the gnarled and aged trees, and crossing and re-crossing from one to the other, netted them together.

Over the creepers again had grown grey-green lichens and long, shaggy moss, so that strands and fringes of it fell on every side, filling the interstices of the gigantic web that stretched from tree to tree, excluding the light of the sun-lit sky.

Beneath, the lower branches of the trees were sad and sodden, overgrown with lichen, clogged with hanging wreaths of moss. A river ran through the wood and at times, swelled by the melting snows, burst, evidently, in roaring flood over its banks.

Everywhere there were traces of recent floods, roots washed bare and places where the swirling waters had heaped up their débris of sticks and mud-stained leaves. All along the damp ground the lowest branches of the trees, weighted with tangled moss, trailed.

broken and bruised by the fierce rush of the current. The trees themselves seemed centuries old, bent and gnarled and twisted into grotesque and ghostly forms. In the dim twilight reigning here one could fancy one stood in some hideous torture-chamber, surrounded by writhing and distorted figures. There an elbow, there a withered arm, a fist clenched in agony, seemed protruding from the sombre, sad-clothed trees, so weirdly knotted and twisted were the old cinder-hued boughs.

As we neared the river we could hear it rushing by long before we could see it, so thick was the under-growth that hung low over it.

It seemed as if we might be approaching the black Styx through this melancholy wood where all seemed weeping in torn veils and ash-coloured garments.

No touch of depression affected my companion; she seemed as insensible to the grey solemnity, the dim mystery of the wood, as she had been to the vivid glory of the sea. She slipped a little velvet hand into mine, and when we drew near to the hidden Styx, murmured softly:

"We will find a dry place, Treevor, on the other side, and sit down among the trees. Then you must take me in your arms and I will be your own Suzee. I do not want my old husband any more."

I stopped and looked down upon her. Not even the

sad light could dim the soft brilliance of her face. It seemed to bloom out of the ashy shadows like an exquisite flower. Her eyes were wells of fire beneath their velvet blackness.

"Do you love me very much?" I asked.

"Oh, yes, so much," she answered with passionate emphasis. "You are so beautiful. Never have I seen any one so beautiful, and so tall and so strong. Oh, it is *pain* to me to love you so much."

And indeed she became quite white, as she drew her hand from mine and clasped both of hers upon her breast as if to still some agony there.

My own heart beat hard. The grey wood seemed to lose its ashy tone and become warm and rosy round us. I bent over her and took her up wholly in my arms, and she laughed and threw hers around me in wild delight.

"Carry me, Treevor, over the bridge and up the slope at the side. It is so nice to feel you carrying me."

It was no difficulty to carry her, and the waves of electricity from her joyous little soul rushed through me till my arms and all the veins of my body seemed alight and burning.

I ran with her, over the narrow bridge and up the slope, where, as she said, there was drier ground. And there, on a bed of leaves under some tangled branches, I fell on my knees with her still clasped to my breast, and covered her small satin-skinned face with kisses.

"I am yours now. You must not let me go. I only want to look and look at your face. I wish I could tell you how I love you. Oh, Treevor, I can't tell you . . ."

As I looked down, breathless with running and kisses and the fires she had kindled within me, I saw how her bosom heaved beneath the yellow jacket, how all the delicate curves of her breast seemed broken up with panting sighs and longing to express in words all that her body expressed so much better.

"Darling, there is no need to tell me. I know." And I put my hand round her soft column of throat, feeling all its quick pulses throbbing hard into the palm of my hand.

"Put your head down on my heart, Treevor. Lie down beside me; now let us think we have drunk a little opium, just a little, and we are going to sleep through a long night together. Hush! What is that? Did you hear anything?"

She lifted my hand from her throat and sat up, listening.

I had not heard anything. I had been too absorbed. All had vanished now from me, except the fervent beauty of the girl before me.

The sea of desire had closed over my head, sealing

the senses to outside things; I drew her towards me impatiently.

"It is nothing," I murmured. "I heard nothing." But she sat up, gazing straight across a small cleared space in front of us to where the impenetrable thicket of undergrowth again stood forward like grey screens between the twisted tree trunks.

"Yes, there was something; there, opposite! Look, something is moving!" I followed her eyes and saw a strand of loose moss quiver and heard a twig break in the quiet round us. We both watched the under-growth across the open space intently. For a second nothing moved, then the boughs parted in front of us, and through the great lichen streamers and rugged bands of grey-green moss depending from them, peered an old, drawn-looking face.

Suzee gave a piercing shriek of dismay, and started to her feet.

"My husband!" she gasped.

I sprang to my feet, and my right hand went to my hip pocket. The head pushed through the thicket, and a bent and aged form followed slowly. I drew out my revolver, but the figure of the old man straightened itself up and he waved his hand impatiently, as if deprecating violence.

"Sir, I have come after my wife," he said, in a low, broken tone.

I slipped the weapon back in my pocket. I had had an idea that he might attack Suzee, but voice and face showed he was in a different mood.

Suzee clung to my hand on her knees, crying and trembling.

"Go and sit over there," he said peremptorily to her, pointing to the other side of the glade, far enough from us to be out of hearing.

She did not move, only clung and shivered and wept as before.

I bent over her, loosening my hand.

"Do as he says," I whispered; "no harm can come to you while I am here."

Suzee let go my fingers reluctantly and crept away, sobbing, to the opposite edge of the thicket. The old Chinaman motioned me to sit down. I did so, mechanically wondering whether his calmness was a ruse under cover of which he would suddenly stab me. He sat down, too, stiffly, beside me, resting on his heels, and his hard, wrinkled hands supporting his withered face.

"Now," he said, in a thin old voice; "look at me! I am an old man, you are a young one. You are strong, you are well; you are rich too, I think." He looked critically over me. "You have everything that I have not, already. Why do you come here to rob an old man of all he has in this world?"

I felt myself colour with anger. All the blood in

my body seemed to rush to my head and stand singing
in my ears.

I felt a furious impulse to knock him aside out of
my way; but his age and weakness held me motionless.

"All my youth, when I was strong and good-looking as you are now, and women loved me, I worked
hard like a slave, and starved and saved. When
others played I toiled, when they spent I hoarded up.
What was I saving for? That I might buy myself
that." He waved his hand in the direction of Suzee,
sitting in a little crumpled heap against a gnarled tree
opposite us.

"I bought her," he went on with increasing excitement. "I bought her from a woman who would have
let her out, night by night, to foreigners. I have given
her a good home, she does no hard work. She has a
child, she has fine clothes. I work still all day and
every day that I may give money to her. She is my
one joy, my treasure; don't take her away from me,
don't do it. You have all the world before you, and
all the women in it that are without husbands. Go to
them, leave me my wife in peace."

Tears were rolling fast down his face now, his clasped
hands quivered with emotion.

"When I was a young man I would not take any
pleasure. No, pleasure means money, and I was saving. When I am old I will buy, I said. It needs

money, when I am old I shall have it. I can buy then. But, ah! when one is old it is all dust and ashes."

I looked at his thin shrunken form, poorly clad, at his face, deeply lined with great furrows, made there by incessant toil and constant pain. I felt my joy in Suzee to wither in the grey shadow of his grief. Some people would have thought him doubtless an immoral old scoundrel, and that he had no business in his old age to try to be happy as younger men are, to wish, to expect it. But I cannot see that joy is the exclusive right of any particular age. A young man or young woman has no more right or title to enjoy than an old man or woman; they have simply the right of might, which is no *right* at all.

"Well, what do you want me to say or do?" I exclaimed impatiently. "Take your wife back with you now, no harm has happened to her. Take her home with you."

"Yes, I can take her body, but not her spirit," answered the old man sadly.

His tone made me look at him keenly. Hitherto I had felt sorry for Suzee that she was his; now, as I heard his accent, I felt sorry for him that he was hers.

A great capacity for suffering looked out of the aged face, such as I knew could never look out of hers.

"If you lift your finger she would come to you!

Promise me you will not see her again, not speak to her; that you will go. And if she comes to you, you will not accept her."

I was silent for a moment.

"My ship goes to-morrow morning," I answered; "I am not likely to see your wife again. I shall not seek her."

"That is not enough," moaned the old man; "she will find a way. She will come to you. Promise me you will not take her away with you; if you do you will have an old man's murder on your head."

I moved impatiently.

"I am not going to take her away," I answered.

"But promise me. If I have your promise I shall feel certain."

I hesitated, and looked across at Suzee, a patch of beautiful colour against the grey background of bent and aged trees.

What had I intended to do, I asked myself. I could not take her, in any case. I had not meant that. A virtuous American ship like the Cottage City would hardly admit a Suzee to share my cabin.

Then what did my promise matter if it but reflected the fact, and if it satisfied him?

"You are not willing to promise," he said, coming close to me and peering into my face; "I feel it."

I thought I heard his teeth close on an unuttered

oath. Still he did not threaten me. As I remained silent he suddenly threw himself on the ground in front of me, and stretched out his hands and put them on my feet.

"Sir, I implore you. Give me your word you will not take her, then I am satisfied. Better take my life than my wife."

I lifted my eyes for a moment in a glance towards Suzee and saw her make a scornful gesture at the prostrate figure. The gold bracelets on her arm below the yellow silk sleeve shewed in the action a contrast to the old, worn clothing of the poorest material that her husband wore.

I rose to my feet and raised him up.

"Get up, I hate to see you kneel to me. I have said I shall not take your wife. As far as I am concerned, that is a promise. I have said it."

"Thank you," he said, inclining his head, and then moved away, not without a certain dignity in his old form, lean and twisted though the work of years had made it.

I dropped back into my place where I had been sitting and watched the two figures before me almost in a dream.

He went up to the girl and spoke, apparently not unkindly, and some talk ensued. Then I saw him bend down and take her wrist and drag her to her feet.

Suzee hung back as one sees a child hang back from a nurse, but she moved forward though unwillingly, and so at last they passed from my sight, through the grey trees and the weeping moss, the thin old man stepping doggedly forward, the pretty, gay-clothed childish little figure dragging back.

Then all was still. The old grey wood was full of weird light, but the silence of the night had fallen on it. Beast and bird and insect had sought their lair and nest and cranny. Not a leaf moved. I felt entirely alone.

"One never knows in life," I thought, repeating my words to Morley.

I felt a keen sense of longing regret surge slowly, heavily through me. How exquisitely sweet and perfect her beauty was! And she had lain in my arms for that moment, one moment that was stamped into my brain in gold. I put my head into my hands and shut out the dim grey wood from vision and recalled that moment. It came back to me, the touch of her soft form, the smiling curve of the lips put up to me, the fire in the liquid depths of those almond eyes, the round throat delicate as polished ivory. The extraordinary triumph of beauty over the senses came before my mind suddenly, presenting the problem that always puzzles and eludes me.

Why should certain lines and colours in pleasing

the eye, so intoxicate and inflame the brain? For it is the brain to which beauty appeals. Youth and health in a loved object are sufficient to capture the physical senses, but they do not fill the brain with that exaltation, that delirium of joy, that divine elation that sweeps up through us at the sight of beauty. Divine fire, it seems to be lighted first in the glance of the eyes.

In an hour's time I left the wood and walked slowly shipwards. I felt tired and overstrained, exceedingly regretful, full of longing after that lovely vision that had come to me and that I had had to drive away.

The unearthly stillness combined with the brilliant, unabated, unfailing light had a curious mystery about it that charmed and delighted me. The sea, so blue and tranquil, sparkled softly on my left hand, the pellucid blue of the sky stretched overhead, and all the air was full of the sweet sunshine we associate with day. Yet it was midnight. I pulled out my watch and looked at it to assure myself of the fact. Sitka was wrapt in silence and sleep, my own footstep resounded strangely in the burning empty streets.

I had to pass the tea-shop on my way to the ship. One could see nothing of it from the street as the compound shut it off from view, and across the compound entrance a stout hurdle was now stretched and barred.

I passed on with a sigh, reached the ship lying mo-

tionless against the quay, went down to my cabin
without encountering any one, threw off my clothes,
and myself in my berth, feeling a sense of fatigue
obliterating thought.

The night before I had had no sleep, and the incessant golden glare, day and night alike, wearies the
nerves not trained to it.

Suzee and almond eyes and injured husbands floated
away from me on the dark wings of sleep.

It must have been an hour or so later that I woke
suddenly with a sense of suffocation. Some soft,
heavy thing lay across my breast. I started up and
two arms clasped my neck and I heard Suzee's voice
saying in my ear:

"Treevor, dear Treevor, I have found you! Now
you will take me away, and we will stay for ever and
ever together. I am so happy."

The cabin was full of the same steady yellow light
as when I closed my eyes. Looking up I saw her
sweet oval face above me.

She was lying on the berth leaning over me, supported
on her elbows.

As I looked up she pressed her lips down on my
face, kissing me on the eyes and mouth with passionate repetition and insistence.

"Dear little girl, dear little Suzee!" I answered,
putting up my arms and folding them round her.

I was only half-awake, and for a moment the old Chinaman was forgotten. It was all rather like a delicious dream.

"I am quite, quite happy now," she said, laying down her head on my chest. "Oh, so happy, Treevor; you must never let me go. I love you so, like this," she added, putting her two hands round my throat, "when I can feel your neck and when you are sleeping. You looked beautiful, just now, when I found you. I am sorry you woke."

Clear consciousness was struggling back now with memory, but not before I had pressed her to me and returned those kisses. She had laid aside her little saffron silk coat, and her breast and arms shone softly through a filmy muslin covering.

I sat up regarding her; very lissom and soft and lovely she looked, and my whole brain swam suddenly with delight.

Surely I could not part with her! She was precious to me in that madness that comes over us at such moments.

I put my arms round her and held her to my breast with all my force in a clasp that must have been painful to her, but she only laughed delightedly.

Then my promise came back to me. It was impossible to break that. What was the good of torturing myself when I had made it impossible to take her. Why had she come here?

"Where is your husband?" I asked mechanically, wondering if any strange fate had removed him from between us.

"Oh, I put him to sleep, he will give no trouble. I gave him opium, so much opium, he will sleep a long time."

"You have not killed him?" I said, in a sudden horror.

Her eyes were wide open and full of extraordinary fire, she seemed in those moments capable of anything.

She put up her little hands and ran them through my hair.

"Such black hair," she murmured. "Ah, how I love it! I love black hair. How it shines, how soft it is! I hate grey hair. It is horrid. No, I have not killed him. He will wake again when we have sailed and are far away from Sitka."

These words drove from me the last veil of clinging sleep. I kept my arms round her and said:

"But, Suzee, I can't take you with me. I promised your husband to-night I would not."

"That's nothing," she replied lightly; "promises are nothing when one loves. And you love me, Treevor; you must love me, and I am coming with you, you can't drive me away."

The ship's bells sounded overhead on deck as she

spoke. The sound seemed a warning. I knew our ship was due to leave in the morning; I did not know quite when. If it left the quay with the girl on board, the horror of a broken promise would cling to me all my life.

"I can't take you, it is impossible. You must go back and try to forget you have ever seen me. You must go now at once, our ship is leaving soon."

"I know," said Suzee tranquilly; "and I shall be so happy when it starts."

I pushed her aside and got up from the berth. The cabin window stood wide open. In the position the ship was it was easy to come in and out through it from the quay. She must have entered that way.

"You must go," I said between my teeth. I was afraid of myself. Overhead I heard movements and clanking chains and shuffling feet. Our ship was leaving, and she was still on board with me.

"Go out of that window now, instantly, or I shall put you out."

"You will not, Treevor," beginning to cry; "you won't be so unkind. I only want to stay with you; let me stay."

She was half-sitting on the edge of my berth, clinging to it with both hands. She was pale with an ivory pallor, her breasts rose in sobs under the transparent muslin of her vest.

73

The ship gave a great heave under our feet.

The blood beat so in my head and round my eyes I could hardly see her. I moved to her, clinging to one blind object. I bent over her and lifted her up. She was like a doll in weight. She was nothing to me.

As she realised my intention she seemed to turn into a wild animal in my arms. She bit and tore at my wrists, and scratched my face with her long sharp nails.

The ship was moving now and I was desperate.

I walked with her to the window and put her feet over the ledge.

We neither of us spoke a word. She clung to my neck so I thought she must overbalance me and drag me through with her.

With all my force I pushed her outwards and away from me. Her hands broke from my neck and scratched down my face till the blood ran from it.

"Don't struggle so," I warned her; "you will drop into the sea if you do." For a blue crack opened already between the moving ship and the quay.

Words were useless. She bit and struggled and clung to me like a cat mad with fear and rage.

With an effort I leant forward and half threw, half dropped her on the woodwork. She fell there with a gasping cry, and I drew the window to and shut it.

The ship rose and fell now and the blue water

gleamed in an ever-widening track between its side and the quay.

I leant against the window glass and watched her through it. She had struggled to her knees and now knelt there weeping and stretching out little ivory tinted hands to the departing ship. My own eyes were full, and only through a mist could I see her kneeling there, a brilliant spot of colour in dazzling light on the deserted quay.

I turned away at last as we struck out on the open water. There, on my berth, facing me as I stumbled back to it, lay a little yellow jacket.

I threw myself upon it and put my hand over my eyes, while the ship made out beyond the fairy islands. And the gold night passed over and melted into the new day.

PART TWO

THE VIOLET NIGHT

CHAPTER IV

AT THE STUDIO

I was back in London again, back in my studio, with the dull grey light of the city falling through the windows, and all the vivid glory, the matchless splendour of the North lay like a past dream in the background of my memory. But still how clear the dream, how bright each moment of it, and how long to my retrospective vision! Was it possible I had only been there three or four months? It seemed like as many years. For time has this peculiarity, that joy and action shorten it while it is passing, but lengthen it when it is past. A week in which we have done nothing of note, but spent in stationary idleness, how long and tedious it seems, yet in looking back upon it, it appears short as a day; while a week in which we have travelled far, seen several cities and been glad in each, though the gilded moments have danced by on lightning feet, when we look back upon that week it seems as if we have lived a year.

It was there, bright, radiant in my mind, the picture of those blue days and golden northern nights, and how the light of the picture seemed to gather round, and centre in a sweet youthful face with the blue stone

76

earrings, hanging against the creamy neck, beside the rounded cheek, and the cluster of red flowers bound on each temple against the smooth black hair!

I settled myself lower in the deep roomy armchair, and pushed my feet forward to the blazing fire. There was still half an hour before I could decently ring for tea, and it was too dark already to work. I had had a hard and disagreeable morning, too, and felt I needed rest and quiet thought. How the red flame leapt in the grate, and what a rich, warm, wine-dark colour it threw all round my red room! I rose and drew the heavy crimson curtains across the windows to shut out their steely patches of grey that spoiled the harmony of colour. I returned to my chair and glanced round with satisfaction. Fitted and furnished and hung with every beautiful shade of red, my studio always delighted and charmed my vision.

My friends said I had papered and furnished it in red to throw up the white limbs and contours of my models, and this had something to do with it, for hardly any colour shows off white flesh to better advantage, though pale blue in this matter runs it close; but this was not the prompting motive. Rather it was that in England where all is so cold and tame and grey, from morals to colours, I liked to surround myself with this glowing barbaric crimson, this warm inviting tint.

My eye in wandering from floor to ceiling rested

77

finally on the empty easel, the numerous white unused sheets of paper near it. I felt in despair. Not even a sketch of a Phryne yet! Not even a model found! Not even the idea of where to find one!

I had been seeing models all the morning, and how wearisome and vexatious, and even, towards the end, how repulsive that becomes! The wearying search after something that corresponds to the perfect ideal in one's brain, the constant raising of hope and ensuing disappointment as a misshapen foot or crooked knee destroys the effect of neck and shoulder, produce at last an intolerable irritation. I had dismissed them all finally, and they had trailed away in the rain, a dismal procession of dark-clothed women.

A quarter of an hour of red stillness in that comfortable room had passed, and the warmth and quiet of it had crept over me and into me, gradually soothing away all vexations, when a knock came on the door and in answer to my, "Come in," some one entered the room behind me.

"I am so glad to find you."

I started to my feet at the sound of the soft voice, and went forward to the door.

"Viola! how good of you to come." I took both her hands and drew her into the firelight which sparkled gratefully on her tall slender figure and the fair waves of hair under her velvet hat.

"May I stay and have tea with you? I have been shopping all the afternoon and as I was driving past I thought I would see if you were in and disengaged."

"I shall be delighted," I said as I wheeled another armchair up to the fire.

"You are sure? You have nothing else to do?"

"Nothing, really nothing," I said, walking to the electric lights and switching them on; "and if I had, I would leave it all to have tea with you."

She laughed, such a pretty dainty laugh! What a contrast to the rough giggles amongst the models this morning!

"Trevor! you are just the same as ever; all compliments. But I am immensely glad you are not going to turn me out, for I am chilly and tired and want my tea and a talk with you very badly." And she settled down in her large chair with a sigh of content.

I came back to the hearth and stood looking down upon her. The light was rose-coloured, falling through tinted globes, and soft as the firelight. She looked exquisite, and she must have seen the admiration in my eyes for she coloured under them.

She was wearing a dark green velvet gown edged with fur and which fitted her lovely figure closely, being perhaps designed to display it.

"You have come like a glorious sunset to a gloomy

day," I said. "I have had a horrid morning and been depressed all the afternoon."

"You have no inspiration, then, yet for the Phryne?" she answered, glancing round; "otherwise you would be in the seventh heaven."

"No," I groaned, "and the models are so dreadful; so far from giving one an inspiration, they would kill any one had. All last week I was trying to find a model, and all this morning again. I would give anything for a good one."

She murmured a sympathetic assent, and I went on, pursuing my own thoughts freely, for Viola was my cousin and no one else knew or understood me so well as she did. We had grown up together, and always talked on all sorts of subjects to each other.

"The difficulty is with most of these English models, they are so thick and heavy, so cart-horsey, or else they are so thin. The tall, graceful ones are too thin. I want those subtle, gracious lines, but I don't want sharp bones and corners. I want smooth, rounded contours, and yet the outlines to be delicate; I want slender grace and suppleness with roundness . . ."

I stopped suddenly, the blood mounting to my forehead. I was looking down at her as she lay back in the chair. She looked at me, and our gaze got locked together. A thought had sprung suddenly between us. I realised all at once I was describing the figure before me, realised that I was face to face with the most perfect, enchanting model of my dearest dreams.

There was a swift rush of red to her face, too, as I stopped. Up till then she had been quietly listening. But she saw my thought then. It was visible to both of us, and for a moment a deadly silence dropped on us. Of course, I ought not to have stopped, but the thought came to me with such a blinding flash of sudden revelation that it paralysed me and took speech from my lips. Just in that moment the door opened and tea was brought in. I turned my attention immediately to making it, and what with asking her how much sugar she would have and pressing her to take hot toast and crumpets, the cloud of embarrassment passed and all was light and easy again. I dismissed the idea instantly, and we did not speak of the picture. I questioned her about her shopping, we recalled the last night's dance where we had been together, and spoke of a hundred other light matters in which we had common interests. Then a silence stole over us, and Viola sank far back in her chair, gazing with absent eyes into the fire.

Suddenly she sat up and turned to me. I saw her heart must be beating fast, for her face and lips had grown quite white.

"Trevor, I wish you would let me be your model for the Phryne."

6   81

Almost immediately she had spoken the colour rushed in a burning stream across her face, forcing the tears to her eyes. I saw them brim up, sparkling to the lids, in the firelight.

I sat up in my chair, leaning forwards towards her. My own heart seemed to rise with a leap into my throat.

"Dearest! I could not think of such a thing! It is so good of you, but . . ."

I stopped. She had sunk back in her chair. She was looking away from me. I saw the tears well up over the lids and roll slowly unchecked down her face.

"I should so like to be of use to you," she murmured in a low tone, "and I think I could be in that way, immense use."

I slid to my knees beside her chair, and took the slim, delicate white hand that hung over the arm in mine and pressed it, very greatly moved and hardly knowing what to answer her.

"I shall never forget you have offered it, never cease to be grateful, but . . ."

"There is no question of being grateful," she broke in gently, "unless it were on my side. I should think it an honour to be made part of your work, to live for ever in it, or at least much longer than in mortal life. What is one's body? It is nothing, it perishes so soon, but what you create will last for centuries at least."

I pressed my lips to her hand in silence. I felt overwhelmed by the suggestion, by the unselfishness, by the grandeur of it. I saw that the proposition stood before her mind in a totally different light from that in which it would present itself to most women. But, then, the outlook of an artist upon life and all the things in life is entirely different from that of the ordinary person. It takes in the wide horizon, it embraces a universe, and not a world, it sweeps up to the large ideals, the abstract form of things, passing over the concrete and the actual which to ordinary minds make up the all they see.

And Viola was an artist: she expressed herself in music as I did in painting. Our temperaments were alike though our gifts were different, and we served the same mystical Goddess though our appointments in her temple were not the same.

As an artist the idea was, to me, simple enough, as a man it horrified me.

"I could not allow it."

She turned upon me.

"Why?" she said simply.

"Well, because . . . because it is too great a sacrifice."

"I have said it is no sacrifice. It is an honour."

"It would injure you if it became known."

"It will not become known."

"Everything becomes known."

"Well, I shouldn't care if it did."

"By and by you might regret it. It might stand in the way of your marrying some one you loved."

"I don't believe I shall ever want to marry. Do I look like a domestic person? In any case, I am quite sure I shouldn't want to marry a man if he objected to my being a model for a great picture to my own cousin. Why, Trevor, we are part of each other, as it were. I am like your own sister. What can it matter? While you are painting me I shall be nothing, the picture will be everything. I am no more than a dream or vision which might come before you, and you will give me life, immortality on your canvas. As an old woman when all beauty has gone from me, I shall be there alive, young, beautiful still."

"It is all sophistry, dearest, I can't do it."

"You will when you have thought it all over," she said softly, "at least if you think I should do—are you sure of that?"

She rose and stood for a moment, one hand outstretched towards the mantelpiece, and resting there for support. The velvet gown clung to her, and almost every line of her form could be followed with the eye or divined. The throat was long, round, and full, the fall of the shoulder and the way its lines melted into the curves of the breast had the very intoxication of beauty in them, the waist was low, slender, and perfect, the main line to the knee and on to the ankle absolutely straight. To my practised eyes the clothing had little concealment. I knew that here was all that I wanted.

"I am supposed to have a very perfect figure," she said with a faint smile, "and it seems rather a pity to use it so little. To let it be of service to you, to give you just what you want, to create a great picture, to save you all further worry over it, which is quite knocking you up, would be a great happiness to me."

She paused. I said nothing.

"I do not think I must stay any longer," she said glancing at my clock, "nor shall I persuade you any more. I leave it entirely in your hands. Write to me if you want me to come. Perhaps you may find another model."

She smiled up at me. Her face had a curious delicate beauty hard to define. The beauty of a very transparent skin and sapphire eyes.

I bent over her and kissed her bright scarlet lips.

"Dearest! if you only knew how I appreciate all you have said, how good I think it of you! And I could never find a lovelier model; you know it is not that thought which influences me, but it is impossible. You must not think of it."

"Very well," she said with a laugh in her lovely eyes, "but *you* will!"

She disengaged herself from me, picked up a fur necklet from her chair, and went to the door.

"Good-night," she said softly, and went out.

Left to myself, I walked restlessly up and down the room. She was right. I could think of nothing but her words to me, and how her visit had changed my mood and all the atmosphere about me! It seemed as if she had filled it with electricity. My pulses were all beating hard. The quiet of the studio was intolerable. I was dining out that evening, and then going on to a dance. I would dress now a little early and then go to the club and spend the intermediate time there.

My bedroom opened out of the studio by a small door, before which I generally had a red and gold Japanese screen. I went in and switched on the light and began to dress, trying to get away from my crowding thoughts.

The temptation to accept Viola's suggestion was the greater because she was so absolutely free and mistress of her own actions.

If she chose of her own free will to do any particular thing there was practically no one else to be consulted and no one to trouble her with reproof or reproaches.

Early left an orphan and in possession of a small fortune in her own right, she had been brought up by an old aunt who simply worshipped her and never questioned nor allowed to be questioned anything which Viola did.

She had given her niece an elaborate education, believing that a girl's mental training should be as severe as a boy's, and Viola knew her Greek and Latin and mathematics better than I knew mine, though all these had lately given way to the study of music, for which she had a great and peculiar gift.

The old lady was delighted when she found her favourite niece was really one of the children of the gods, as she put it, and henceforth Viola's life was left still more unrestrained.

"She has genius, Trevor," she would say to me, "just as you have, and we ordinary people can't profess to guide or control those who in reality are so much greater than we are. I leave Viola to judge for herself about life, I always have since she was quite a little thing, and I have no fear for her. Whatever she does I know it will always be right."

Viola was just twenty, but this kind of training had given her an intelligence and developed her intellect far beyond her years.

In her outlook upon life she was more like a man than a woman, and, never having been to school nor mixed much with other girls of her own age, she was free from all those small, petty habits of mind, that littleness of mental vision that so mars and dwarfs the ordinary feminine character.

In this question of posing for the picture, to take her face also would, of course, be quite impossible, but I had my own ideal for the Phryne's face, nor was that important.

That the figure should be something of unusual beauty, something peculiarly distinctive seemed to me a necessity. For the form of the Grecian Phryne had, by the mere force of its perfect and triumphant beauty, swept away the reason of all that circle of grey-bearded hostile judges called upon to condemn it, had carved for itself a place in history for ever. There should in its presentment be something peculiarly arresting and enchanting, or the artistic idea, the spirit of the picture, would be lost.

The next morning I interviewed models again, and so strange is the human mind that while I honestly tried to find one that suited me, tried to be satisfied, I was full of feverish apprehension that I might do so, and when I had seen the last and could with perfect honesty reject her, I felt a rush of extraordinary elation all through me. I knew, and told myself so, every half second, that Viola's temptation was one I ought to and must resist, and yet the idea of yielding filled me with a wild instinctive delight that no reason could suppress. Yes, because once an artist has seen or conceived by his own imagination his perfect ideal, nothing else, nothing short of this will satisfy him. If it was difficult for me to find a model before, it was practically impossible to do so now. For, having once realised what it wanted, the mind impatiently rejected everything else, though it might possibly have accepted something less than its desire before that realisation of it.

These models were all well-formed women, but they were commonplace. The hold Viola's form had upon the eye was that it was not commonplace. Its beauty was distinctive, peculiar, arresting. I was not a painter of types, but of exceptions. The common things of life are not interesting, nor do I think they are worthy subjects for Art to concern itself with. Something unusually beautiful, transcending the common type, is surely the best for the artist to try to perpetuate.

Friday came, the end of the week, and I was still without a model. My nights had been nearly sleepless, and my days full of feverish anxiety: an active anxiety to accept another sitter and withstand the temptation of Viola, which fought desperately with the more passive anxiety not to be satisfied and to be obliged to yield. Between these two I had grown thin, as they fought within me, tearing me in the struggle.

To-day, Friday, the war was over. I had sent a note to Viola asking her to have tea with me. If she came, if she still held to her wish, I should accept, and the Phryne was assured. How my heart leapt at the thought! Those last hours before an artist gives the first concrete form to the brain children of his intangible dreams, how full of a double life he seems! I was back from lunch and in the studio early; I could not tell when she might come, and I closed all the windows and made up the fire till the room seemed like a hot-house. I arranged a dais with screens of flaming colour behind it reflecting the red rays of the fire.

If she consented, she should stand here after having changed into the Greek dress. And as the moment chosen for the picture was that in which Phryne is unveiling herself before her judges, I intended to let her discard the drapery as she liked. I should not attempt to pose her; I would not even direct her; I should simply watch her, and at some moment during the unveiling she would fall naturally into just the pose—some pose—I did not know myself yet which might give me my inspiration—that I wished. Then I would arrest her, ask her to remain in it. I thought so we should arrive nearest to the effect of that famous scene of long ago.

The dress I had chosen was of a dull red tint, not unlike that of Leighton's picture, but I had no fear of seeming to copy Leighton. What true artist ever fears he may be considered a copyist? He knows the strength and vitality of his conception will need no spokesman when it appears.

I felt frightfully restless and excited, a mad longing filled me to get the first sketch on paper. I hardly thought of Viola as Viola or my cousin then. She was already the Phryne of Athens for me, but when suddenly a light knock came on the door outside my heart seemed to stand still and I could hardly find voice to say, "Come in." When she entered, dressed in her modern clothes and hat, and held out her hand, all the modern, mundane atmosphere came back and brought confusion with it.

"You said come early, so here I am," she said lightly. "Trevor," she added, gazing at me closely, "you are looking awfully handsome, but so white and ill. What is the matter?"

"I have been utterly wretched about the picture. I know I ought not to accept your offer, but the temptation is too great. If you feel the same as you did about it, I am going to ask you to pose for me this afternoon."

"I do feel just the same, Trevor," she answered earnestly. "You can't think how happy and proud I am to be of use to you."

"You know what the picture is?" I asked her,

holding her two hands and looking down into the great eyes raised confidently to mine.

"I want you to dress in all those red draperies, and then, standing on the dais, to drop them, let them fall from you."

"Yes, I think I know exactly. I will try, and, if I don't do it rightly, you must tell me and we must begin again."

She took off her hat and cloak and gloves. Then she turned to me and asked for the dress. I gave it to her and showed her how it fastened and unfastened with a clasp on the shoulder.

She listened quietly to my directions, then, gathering up all the thin drapery, walked to the screen and disappeared from my view.

I sat down waiting. A great nervous tension held me. I had ceased to think of the right or wrong of my action. I was too absorbed now in the thought of the picture to be conscious of anything else.

When she came from behind the screen clothed in the red Athenian draperies her face was quite white, but composed and calm. She did not look at me, but walked to the platform at once. I had withdrawn to a chair as far from it as was practicable, divining that the nearer I was the more my presence would weigh upon her. She faced me now on the dais, and very slowly began to unfasten the buckle on her shoulder. I sat watching her intently, hardly breathing, waiting for the moment.

She was to me nothing now but the Phryne, and I was nothing but a pencil held in the hand of Art.

The first folds of crimson fell, disclosing her throat and shoulders, the others followed, piling softly one on the other to her waist, where they stayed held by her girdle. The shoulders and breasts were revealed exquisite, gleaming white against the dull glow of the crimson stuff. I waited. It was a lovely, entrancing vision, but I waited. She lowered her hand from her shoulder and brought it to her waist, firmly and without hesitation she unclasped the belt, and then taking the sides of it, one in each hand, with its enclosed drapery, which parted easily in the centre, she made a half step forwards to free herself from it, and stood revealed from head to foot. It was the moment. Her head thrown up, with her eyes fixed far above me, her throat and the perfect breast thrown outwards and forwards, the slight bend at the slim waist accentuating the round curves of the hips, one straight limb with the delicate foot advanced just before the other, the arms round, beautifully moulded, held tense at her sides, as the hands clutched tightly the falling folds behind her, these made up the physical pose, and the pride, the tense nervousness, the defiance of her own feelings gave its meaning expression. I raised my hand and called to her to pause just so, to be still, if she could, without stirring.

She quivered all through her frame at the sudden shock of hearing my voice; then stood rigid. I had my paper ready, and began to sketch rapidly.

How beautiful she was! In all my experience, in the whole of my career, I had never had such a model. The skin was a marvellous whiteness: there seemed no brown, red, or yellow shades upon it; nor any of that mottled soap appearance that ruins so many models. She was white, with the warm, true dazzling whiteness of the perfect blonde.

My head burned: I felt that great wave of inspiration roll through me that lifts the artist to the feet of heaven. There is no happiness like it. No, not even the divine transports and triumph of love can equal it.

I sketched rapidly, every line fell on the paper as I wished it. The time flew. I felt nothing, knew nothing, but that the glorious image was growing, taking life under my hand. I was in a world of utter silence, alone with the spirit of divine beauty directing me, creating through me.

Suddenly, from a long distance it seemed, a little cry or exclamation came to me.

"Trevor, I must move!"

I started, dropped the paper, and rose.

The light had grown dim, the fire had burned hollow.

Viola had dropped to her knees, and was for the moment a huddled blot of whiteness amongst the crimson tones. I advanced, filled with self-reproach for my selfish absorption. But she rose almost directly, wrapped in some of the muslin, and walked from the dais to the screen. I hesitated to follow her there, and went back to the fallen picture. I picked it up and gazed on it with rapture—how perfect it was! The best thing of a lifetime! Viola seemed so long behind the screen I grew anxious and walked over to it. As I came round it, she was just drawing on her bodice, her arms and neck were still bare. She motioned me back imperatively, and I saw the colour stream across her face. I retreated. It was absurd in a way, that blush as my eyes rested on her then, I who just now ... and yet perfectly reasonable, understandable. Then she was the Phryne, a vision to me, as she had said, in ancient Athens. And now we were modern man and woman again. All that we do in this life takes its colour from our attitude of mind towards it, and but for her artist's mind, a girl like Viola could never have done what she had at all.

In a moment more she came from behind the screen. She looked white and cold, and came towards the fire shivering. I drew her into my arms, strained her against my breast, and kissed her over and over again in a passion of gratitude.

"How can I thank you! You have done for me what no one else could. I can never tell you what I feel about it."

She put her arms round my neck, and kissed me in return.

"Any one would do all they could for you, I think," she said softly. "You are so beautiful and so nice about things I am only too happy to have been of use to you."

"What a brute I was to have forgotten you were standing so long. Was it very bad? Were you cold?"

"At the end I was, but I shouldn't have moved for that. I got so cramped. I couldn't keep my limbs still any longer. I was sorry to be so stupid and have to disturb you."

"I can't think how you stood so well," I said remorsefully, "and so long. It is so different for a practised model."

"Well, I did practise keeping quite still in one position every day all this last week, but of course a week is not long."

I had pressed the bell, and tea was brought in. I busied myself with making it for her. She looked white and ill. I felt burning with a sense of elation, of delighted triumph. The picture was there. It glimmered a white patch against the chair a little way off. The idea was realised, the inspiration caught, all the rest was only a matter of time.

We drank our tea in silence. Viola looked away from me into the fire. She did not seem constrained or embarrassed. Having decided to do, as she had, and conquer her own feelings, she did so simply, grandly, in a way that suited the greatness of her nature. There was no mincing modesty, no self-conscious affectation. The agony of confusion that she had felt in that moment when she had stood before me with her hand on the clasp of her girdle, had been evident to me, but her pride forced her to crush it out of sight.

I went over to her low chair and sat down at her feet.

"Do you know you have shown me this afternoon something which I did not believe existed—an absolutely perfect body without a fault or flaw anywhere. I did not believe there could be anything so exquisitely beautiful."

She coloured, but a warm happy look came into her eyes as she gazed back at me.

"So I did really satisfy you? I realised your expectations?" she murmured. I lifted one of her hands to my lips and kissed it.

"Satisfied is not the word," I returned, looking up into the dark blue eyes above me with my own burning with admiration. "I was entranced. May I shew it to you?"

"Yes, I should like to see it," she answered.

I rose and brought over to her the picture and set

it so that we both could see it together. She gazed at it some time in silence.

"Do you like it?" I asked suddenly with keen anxiety.

"You have idealised me, Trevor!"

"It is impossible to idealise what is in itself divine," I replied quietly. She looked at me, her face full of colour but her eyes alight and smiling.

"I am so glad, so happy that you are pleased. You have drawn it magnificently. What life you put into your things—they live and breathe."

She turned and looked at my clock.

"I must go now, I have been here ages." She began to put on her hat and cloak. When I had fastened the latter round her throat, I took both her hands in mine.

"May I expect you to-morrow?"

"To-morrow? Let me see. Well, I was going to the Carrington's to lunch. I promised to go, so I must; but I need not stay long. I can leave at three and be here at half past; only that will be too late in any case on account of the light, won't it?"

"Not if it is a bright day."

"You see, I need not accept any more invitations. I shan't, if I am coming here, but I have one or two old engagements I must keep."

I dropped her hands and turned away.

"But I can't let you give up your amusements, your time for me in this way!" I said.

Viola laughed.

"It's not much to give up—a few luncheons and teas! As long as I have time for my music I will give you all the rest."

She stood drawing on her gloves, facing the fire; her large soft, fearless eyes met mine across the red light.

I stepped forwards towards her impulsively.

"What *can* I say? How can I thank you or express a hundredth part of my gratitude?"

Viola shook her head with her softest smile and a warm caressing light in her eyes.

"You look at it quite wrongly," she said lightly. "My reward is great enough, surely! You are giving me immortality."

Then she went out, and I was alone.

For a fortnight I was happy. Viola came regularly every day to the studio, and the picture grew rapidly, I was absorbed in it, lived for it, and had that strange peace and glowing content that Art bestows, and which like that other peace "passeth all understanding."

Then gradually a sense of unrest mingled with the calm. The whole afternoon while Viola was with me I worked happily, content to the point of being absolutely oblivious of everything except ourselves and the picture. Our tea together afterwards, when we discussed the progress made and the colour effects, was a delight. But the moment the door was closed after her, when she had left me, a blank seemed to spread round me. The picture itself could not console me. I gazed and gazed at it, but the gaze did not satisfy me nor soothe the feverish unrest. I longed for her presence beside me again.

One day after the posing she seemed so tired and exhausted that I begged her to lie down a little and drew up my great comfortable couch, like a Turkish divan, to the fire. She did as she was bid, and I heaped up a pile of blue cushions behind her fair head.

"I am so tired," she exclaimed and let her eyes close and her arms fall beside her.

I stood looking down on her. Her face was shell-like in its clear fairness and transparency, and the beautiful expressive eyebrows drawn delicately on the white forehead appealed to me.

The intimacy established between us, her complete willing sacrifice to me, her surrender, her trust in me, the knowledge of herself and her beauty she had allowed me gave birth suddenly in my heart to a great overwhelming tenderness and a necessity for its expression.

I bent over her, pressed my lips down on hers and held them there. She did not open her eyes, but raised her arms and put them round my neck, pressing me to her. In a joyous wave of emotion I threw myself beside her and drew the slender, supple figure into my arms.

"Trevor," she murmured, as soon as I would let her, "I am afraid you are falling in love with me."

"I have already," I answered. "I love you, I want you for my own. You must marry me, and come and live at the studio."

"I don't think I can marry you," she replied in very soft tones, but she did not try to move from my clasp.

"Why not?"

"Artists should not marry: it prevents their development. How old are you?"

"Twenty-eight," I answered, half-submerged in the delight of the contact with her, of knowing her in my arms, hardly willing or able to listen to what she said.

"And how many women have you loved?"

"Oh, I don't know," I answered. "I have been with lots, of course, but I don't think I have ever loved at all till now."

"What about the little girl in the tea-shop at Sitka?"

"I don't think I loved her. I wanted her as an experience."

"Is it not just the same with me?"

"No, it isn't. It's quite different. Do not worry me with questions, Viola. Kiss me and tell me you love me."

She raised herself suddenly on one elbow and leant

over me, kissing me on the eyes and lips, all over my face, with passionate intensity.

"I do love you. You are like my life to me, but I know I ought not to marry you. I should absorb you. You would love me. You would not want to be unfaithful to me. But fidelity to one person is madness, an impossibility to an artist if he is to reach his highest development. It can't be. We must not think of it."

The blood went to my head in great waves. The supreme tenderness of a moment back seemed gone, her words had roused another phase of passion, the harsh fury of it.

"I don't care about the art, I don't care about anything. You shall marry me. I will make you love me."

"You don't understand. If you were fifty-eight I would marry you directly."

"You shall marry me before then," I answered, and kissed her again and put my hands up to her soft-haired head to pull it down to my breast and dragged loose some of its soft coils.

"Trevor, you are mad. Let me get up."

I rose myself, and left her free to get up. She sat up on the couch, white and trembling.

"Now you are going to say you won't come to me any more, I suppose?" I said angrily. The nervous excitement of the moment was so great; there was such a wild booming in my ears I could hardly hear my own voice.

She looked up. The tears welled into her luminous blue eyes.

"How unkind you are! and how unjust! Of course I shall come, must come every day if you want it till the Phryne is done. You don't know how I love you."

I took her dear little hand and kissed it.

"I am sorry," I said. "Forgive me, but you must not say such stupid things. Of course you will marry me; why, we are half married already. Most people would say we ought to be."

I turned on the lights and drew the table up to the fire, which I stirred, and began to make the tea.

Viola sat on the edge of the couch in silence, coiling up her hair.

She seemed very pale and tired, and I tried to soothe her with increased tenderness. I made her a cup of tea and came and sat beside her while she drank it. Then I put my arm round her waist and got her to lean against me, and put her soft fair-haired head down on my shoulder and rest there in silence.

I stroked one of her hands that lay cold and nerveless in her lap with my warm one.

"You have done so much for me," I said softly; "wonderful things which I can never forget, and now you must belong to me altogether. No two people could love each other more than we do. It would be absurd of us not to marry." I kissed her, and she accepted my caresses and did not argue with me any more; so I felt happier, and when she rose to leave our good-bye was very tender, our last kiss an ecstasy.

When she had gone I picked up one of the sketches I had first made of her and gazed long at it.

How extravagantly I had come to love her now. I realised in those moments how strong this passion was that had grown up, as it were, under cover of the work, and that I had not fully recognised till now.

How intensely the sight of these wonderful lines moved me! I felt that I could worship her, literally. That she had become to me as a religion is to the enthusiast.

I must be the possessor, the sole owner of her. I felt she was mine already. The agony and the loss, if she ever gave herself to another, would be unendurable. If that happened I should let a revolver end everything for me. I did not believe even the thought of my work would save me.

Yet how curious this same passion is, I reflected, gazing at the exquisite image on the paper before me. If one of these lines were bent out of shape, twisted, or crooked, this same passion would cease to be. The love and affection and esteem I had for her would remain, but this intense desire and longing for her to be my own property, which shook me now to the very depths of my system, would utterly vanish.

Yet it would be wrong to say that these lines alone had captured me, for had they enclosed a stupid or commonplace mind they would have stirred me as little as if they themselves had been imperfect.

No, it is when we meet a Spirit that calls to us from within a form of outward beauty, and only then, that the greatest passion is born within us.

And that I felt for Viola now, and I knew—looking back through a vista of other and lighter loves—I had never known yet its equal. She loved me, too, that great fact was like a chord of triumphant music ringing through my heart. Then why this fancy that she would not marry me? How could I possibly break it down? persuade her of its folly?

I walked up and down the studio all that evening, unable to go out to dinner, unable to think of anything but her, and all through the night I tossed about, restless and sleepless, longing for the hour on the following day which should bring her to me again.

Yet how those hours tried me now! It would be impossible to continue. She must and should marry me. It was only for me she held back from it apparently, yet for me it would be everything.

One afternoon, after a long sitting, the power to work seemed to desert me suddenly. My throat closed nervously, my mouth grew dry, the whole room seemed swimming round me, and the faultless, dazzling figure before me seemed receding into a darkening mist. I flung away my brush and rose suddenly. I felt I must move, walk about, and I started to pace the room, then suddenly reeled, and saved myself by clutching at the mantelpiece.

"What is it? What is the matter?" came Viola's voice, sharp with anxiety, across the room. "Are you ill? Shall I come to you?"

"No, no," I answered, and put my head down on the mantelpiece. "Go and dress. I can't work any more."

I heard her soft slight movements as she left the dais. I did not turn, but sank into the armchair beside me, my face covered by my hands.

Screens of colour passed before my eyes, my ears sang.

I had not moved when I felt her come over to me. I looked up, she was pale with anxiety.

"You are ill, Trevor! I am so sorry."

"I have worked a little too much, that's all," I said constrainedly, turning from her lovely anxious eyes.

"Have you time to stay with me this evening? We could go out and get some dinner, if you have, and then go on to a theatre. Would they miss you?"

"Not if I sent them a wire. I should like to stay with you. Are you better?"

I looked up and caught one of her hands between my own burning and trembling ones.

"I shall never be any better till I have you for my own, till we are married. Why are you so cruel to me?"

"Cruel to you? Is that possible?" Her face had crimsoned violently, then it paled again to stone colour.

"Well, don't let's discuss that. The picture's done. I can't work on it any more. It can't be helped. Let's go out and get some dinner, anyway."

Viola was silent, but I felt her glance of dismay at the only half-finished figure on the easel.

She put on her hat and coat in silence, and we went out. After we had ordered dinner and were seated before it at the restaurant table we found we could not eat it. We sat staring at one another across it, doing nothing.

"Did you really mean that . . . that you wouldn't finish the picture?" she said, after a long silence.

I looked back at her; the pale transparency of her skin, the blue of the eyes, the bright curls of her hair in the glow of the electric lamp, looked wonderfully delicate, entrancing, and held my gaze.

"I don't think I can. I have got to a point where I must get away from it and from you."

"But it is dreadful to leave it unfinished."

"It's better than going mad. Let's have some champagne. Perhaps that will give us an appetite."

Viola did not decline, and the wine had a good effect upon us.

We got through some part of our dinner and then took a hansom to the theatre. As we sat close, side by side, in one of the dark streets, I bent over her and whispered:

"If we had been married this morning, and you were coming back to the studio with me after the theatre I should be quite happy and I could finish the picture."

She said nothing, only seemed to quiver in silence, and looked away from me out of the window.

We took stalls and had very good seats, but what that play was like I never knew. I tried to keep my eyes on the stage, but it floated away from me in waves of light and colour. I was lost in wondering where I had better go to get fresh inspiration, to escape from the picture, from Viola, from myself. Away, I must get away. *Cœlum, non animum, mutant qui trans mare current* is not always true. Our mind is but a chameleon and takes its hues from many skies.

In the vestibule at the end I said:

"It's early yet. Come and have supper somewhere with me, you had a wretched dinner."

Anything to keep her with me for an hour longer! Any excuse to put off, to delay that frightful wrench that seems to tear out the inside of both body and soul which parting from her to-night would mean.

"Do you want me to come to the studio with you afterwards?" she asked.

I looked back at her with my heart beating violently. Her face was very pale, and the pupils in her eyes dilated.

We had moved through the throng and passed outside.

The night was fine. We walked on, looking out for a disengaged hansom. I could hardly breathe: my heart seemed stifling me. What was in her mind? What would the next few minutes mean for us both?

My brain swam. My thoughts went round in dizzying circles.

"We shan't have time for supper and to go to the studio as well," I answered quietly.

"I don't think I want any supper," she replied.

A sudden joy like a great flame leapt through me as I caught the words.

A crawling hansom came up. I hailed it and put her in and sprang in beside her, full of that delight that touches in its intensity upon agony. "Westbourne Street," I called to the man. "No. 2, The Studio."

CHAPTER V

THE CALL OF THE CUCKOO

I STOOD looking through the window of my studio thinking.

The worst had happened, or the best, whichever it was. Viola had become my mistress. She had resolutely refused to be my wife, and the alternative had followed of necessity. The picture had brought us together, it held us together. I could not separate from her without sacrificing the picture, and so destroying her happiness, as she said, and rendering useless all that she had done for me so far.

The picture forced us into an intimacy from which I could not escape and which, now that the devastating clutch of passion had seized me, I could not endure unless she became my own. Viola had seen this and given me herself as unhesitatingly as she had at first given me her beauty for the picture.

In her relations with me she seemed to reach the highest point of unselfishness possible to the human character. For I felt that it was to me and for me she had surrendered herself, not to her own passion nor for her own pleasure.

She would have come day after day and sat to me, shewed me herself and delighted in that self's-reproduction on the canvas, talked to me, delighted in our common worship of beauty, accepted my caresses and—for herself—wanted nothing more.

I had worked well in the past fortnight since the night of the theatre, not so well perhaps as in that first clear period of inspiration, of purely artistic life when Viola was to me nothing but the beautiful Greek I was creating on my canvas, but still, well.

Some may think I naturally should from a sense of gratitude, a sense of duty,—that I should be spurred to do my best, since avowedly Viola had sacrificed all that the work should be good.

But ah, how little has the Will to do with Art!

How well has the German said, "The Will in morals is everything; in Art, nothing. In Art, nothing avails but the being able."

The most intense desire, the most fervid wish, in Art, helps us nothing. On the contrary, a great desire to do well in Art, more often blinds the eye and clogs the brain and causes our hand to lose its cunning. Unbidden, unasked for, unsought, often in our lightest, most careless moments, the Divine Afflatus descends upon us.

We had arranged to have a week-end together out of town. Fate had favoured us, for Viola's aunt had gone to visit her sister for a few weeks, and the girl was left alone in the town house, mistress of all her time and free to do as she pleased.

The short interviews at the studio, delightful as they were, seemed to fail to satisfy us any longer. We craved for that deeper intimacy of "living together."

This is supposed to be fatal to passion in the end, but whether this is so or not, it is what passion always demands and longs for in the beginning.

So we had planned for four days together in the country, four days of May, with a delicious sense of delight and secret joy and warm heart-beatings.

I had dined at her house last night when all the final details had been arranged in a palm-shaded corner by the piano, our conversation covered by the chatter of the other guests. No one knew of our plan, it was a dear secret between us, but it would not have mattered very much if others had known that we were going into the country. I was always supposed to be able to look after Viola, and everybody assumed that it was only a question of time when we should marry each other. We had grown up together, we were obviously very much attached to each other, and we were cousins. And with that amazing inconsistency that is the chief feature of the British public, while it would be shocked at the idea of your marrying your sister, it always loves the idea of your marrying your cousin, the person who in all the world is most like your sister.

However, all we as hapless individuals of this idiotic community have to do is to secretly evade its ridiculous conventions when they don't suit us, and to make the most of them when they do.

And as I was more anxious to marry Viola than about anything else in the world, I welcomed the convention that assigned her to me and made the most of it.

For all that, we kept the matter of our four days to ourselves and planned out its details with careful secrecy.

I was to meet her at Charing-Cross station, and we were going to take an afternoon train down into Kent where Viola declared she knew of a lovely village of the real romantic kind. I had thought we ought to write or wire for rooms at a hotel beforehand, but Viola had been sure she would find what she wanted when we arrived, and she wished to choose a place herself.

So there was nothing more to do. My suit-case was packed, and when the time came to a quarter past two I got into a hansom and drove to the station.

Almost as soon as I got there, Viola drove up, punctual to the minute.

She knew her own value to men too well to try and enhance it by always being late for an appointment as so many women do.

She looked fresh and lovely in palest grey, her rose-tinted face radiant with excitement.

"I haven't kept you waiting, have I?" was her first exclamation after our greeting.

"I had so much work to do for Aunt Mary all the morning, I thought I should not have time to really get off myself."

"No, you haven't kept me waiting," I answered; "and, if you had, it would not have mattered. You know I would wait all day for you."

She glanced up with a wonderful light-filled smile that set every cell in my body singing with delight, and we went down the platform to choose our carriage.

When the train started from Charing Cross the day was dull and heavy-looking, warm, without sunshine. But after an hour's run from town we got into an atmosphere of crystal and gold and the Kentish fruit trees stretched round us a sea of pink and white foam under a cloudless sky.

When we stepped out at our destination, a little sleepy country station, the air seemed like nectar to us. It was the breath of May, real merry, joyous English May at the height of her wayward, uncertain beauty.

We left our light luggage at the station, and walked out from it, choosing at random the first white, undulating road that opened before us.

The little village clustered round the station, but Viola did not want to lodge in the village.

"We can come back to it if we are obliged, but we shall be sure to find a cottage or a wayside inn."

So we went on slowly in the transparent light of a perfect May afternoon.

There are periods when England both in climate and landscape is perfect, when her delicate, elusive loveliness can compare favourably with the barbaric glory, the wild magnificence of other countries.

On this afternoon a sort of rapture fell upon us both as we went down that winding road. The call of the cuckoo resounded from side to side, clear and sonorous like a bell, it echoed and re-echoed across our path under the luminous dome of the tranquil sky and over the hedges of flowering thorn, snow-white and laden with fragrance.

Everywhere the fruit trees were in bloom: delicate masses of white and pink rose against the smiling innocent blue of the sky.

"Now here is the very place," exclaimed Viola suddenly, and following her eyes I saw behind the high, green hedge bordering the road on which we were walking some red roofs rising, half hidden by the masses of white cherry blossom which hung over them. A cottage was there boasting a garden in front, a garden that was filled with lilac and laburnum not yet in bloom; filled to overflowing, for the lilac bulged all over the hedge in purple bunches and the laburnum poured its young leaves down on it. A tiny lawn, rather long-grassed and not innocent of daisies, took up the centre of the garden, and on to this two open casements looked; above again, two open windows, half-lost in the white clouds of cherry bloom.

"But how do you know they've any rooms?" I expostulated.

Viola looked at me with jesting scorn in her eyes.

"I don't know yet, but I'm going to find out."

She put her hand unhesitatingly on the latch of this apparently sacred domain of a private house, opened the gate, and passed in; I followed her inwardly fearful of what our reception might be.

"Men have no moral courage," she remarked superbly as we reached the porch and rang the bell.

A clean-looking woman came to the door after some seconds.

"Apartments? Yes, miss, we have a sitting-room and two bedrooms vacant," she answered to Viola's query. "Shall I show them to you?"

We passed through a narrow, little hall smelling of new oilcloth into a fair-sized room which possessed one of the casements we had seen from outside and through which came the white glow and scent of the cherry bloom and the song of a thrush.

"This will do," remarked Viola with a glance round; "and what bedrooms have you? We only want a sitting-room and one bedroom now."

"Well, ma'am, the room over this is the drawing-room. That's let from next Monday. Then I have a nice double-room, however, I could let with this."

"We will go and see it," said Viola. And we went upstairs.

It seemed a long way up, and when we reached it and the door was thrown open we saw a large room, it was true, but the ceiling sloped downwards at all sorts of unexpected angles like that of an attic, and the casements were small, opening almost into the branches of the cherry-tree.

"What do you want for these two?" Viola enquired.

"Five guineas a week, ma'am," returned the woman, placidly folding her hands together in front of her.

I saw a momentary look of surprise flash across Viola's face. Even she, the young person of independent wealth, and who commanded far more by her talents, was taken aback at the figure.

"Surely that's a good deal," she said after a second.

"Well, ma'am, I had an artist here last summer and he had these two rooms, and he said as he was leaving: 'Mrs. Jevons, you can't ask too much for these rooms. The view from that window and the cherry-tree alone is worth all the money.'"

We glanced through the window as she spoke. It was certainly very lovely. A veil of star-like jasmine hung at one side, and without, through the white bloom of the cherry, one caught glimpses of the turquoise-blue of the sky. Beneath, the garden with the wandering thrushes and its masses of lilac; beyond, the soft outline of the winding country road leading to indefinite distance of low blue hills.

"We'll take them for the sake of the cherry-tree," Viola said smiling.

"Will you send to the station for our light luggage and let us have some tea presently?"

The woman promised to do both at once and ambled out of the room, leaving us there and closing the door behind her.

I looked round, a sense of delight, of spontaneous joy, filling slowly every vein, welling up irresistibly all through my being.

For the first time I stood in a room with Viola which we were going to share. No other form of possession, of intimacy, is quite the same as this, nor speaks to a lover in quite the same way.

I looked at her. She stood in the centre of the rather poorly furnished and bare-looking room, in her travelling dress of a soft grey cloth. Her figure that always woke all my senses to rapture, shewed well in the clear, simple lines of the dress. Over the perfect bosom passed little silver cords, drawing the coat to meet.

Beneath her grey straw summer hat, wide-brimmed, a pink rose nestled against the light masses of her hair. Her eyes looked out at me with a curious, tender smile.

She threw herself into a low cane chair by the window, and I crossed the room suddenly and knelt beside it.

"Darling, you are pleased to be here with me, are you not?"

"Pleased! I am absolutely happy. I have the sensation that whatever happened I could not possibly be more happy than I am."

She put one arm round my neck and went on softly in a meditative voice:

"I can't think how some girls go on living year after year all through their youth never knowing this sort of pleasure and happiness, for which they are made, can you?"

"They don't dare to do the things, I suppose," I answered.

"Perhaps they wouldn't give them any pleasure, . . . but it seems extraordinary." Her voice died away. Her blue eyes fixed themselves on me in a soft, dreaming gaze.

I locked both my arms round her waist and kissed her lips into silence. A knock at the door made me spring to my feet. Viola remained where she was, unmoved, and said, "Come in."

A trim-looking maid came in with rather round eyes fixed open to see all she could. She had a can of hot water in her hand.

"Please, mum, I thought you'd like some hot water."

"Very much," returned Viola calmly. "Thank you."

The maid very slowly crossed the room to the washing-stand and set the can in the basin, covering it with a towel with elaborate care and deliberateness, looking at Viola out of the corners of her eyes as she did so.

"Please, m'm, when your luggage comes shall I bring it up?"

"Yes, do please, bring it up at once," replied Viola, and the girl slowly withdrew, shutting the door in the same lengthy manner after her.

Viola got up and crossed to the glass. She took off her hat and smoothed back her hair with her hand. Each time she did so, the light rippled exquisitely over its shining waves.

"I wonder if I ought to wash my face?" she remarked, looking in the glass; "does it look dusty?"

"Not in the least," I said, studying the pink and white reflection in the glass over her shoulder.

"Don't waste the time washing your face. Come and look out of the window."

We went over to the little casement, and leant our arms side by side on the sill.

The glorious afternoon sunlight was ripening and deepening into orange, a burnished sheen lay over everything, the blue hills were changing into violet, the trees along the road stood motionless, soft, and feathery-looking in the sleepy heat. As we looked out we saw a light cart coming leisurely along and recognised our luggage in it.

Some fifteen minutes later the round-eyed maid reappeared, with a man following her carrying our luggage.

"If you please, m'm, Mrs. Jevons says would the gentleman go down and give what orders he likes for dinner for to-day and to-morrow as the tradesmen are here now and would like to know."

"Do you mind going down, Trevor?" Viola asked me. "I want just to get a few of my things out?"

"Certainly not," I answered, "I'll go." And I followed the maid out and downstairs.

When I returned to the room about half-an-hour later, it was empty, and as I looked round it seemed transformed, now that her possessions were scattered about. I walked across it, a curious sense of pleasure seeming to clasp my heart and rock it in a cradle of joy.

I glanced at the toilet table. On the white cloth lay now two gold-backed brushes, a gold-backed mirror and a gold button-hook, a little clock in silver and a framed photograph of me; over the chair by the dressing-table was thrown what seemed a mass of mauve silk and piles of lace. I lifted it very gently, fearing it would almost fall to pieces, it seemed so fragile, and discovered it was her dressing-gown. How the touch of its folds stirred me since it was *hers!*

I replaced it carefully, wondering at the keen sensation of pleasure that invaded me as the soft laces touched my hands.

I turned to my own suit-case, unstrapped it, opened it, and then pulled out the top drawer of the chest, intending to lay my things in, but I stopped short as I drew it out.

A sheet of tissue paper lay on the top, and underneath this was her dinner-dress—a delicate white cloud of shimmering stuff told me it was that—and at the end of the drawer I saw two little white shoes and white silk stockings.

I paused, looking down at the contents of the drawer, wondering at the wave of emotion they sent through me. Why, when I possessed the girl herself, should these things of hers have any power to move me?

It was perhaps partly because this form of possession, of intimacy, was so new to me, and partly because I was young and still keenly sensitive to all the delights of life and not yet even on the edge of satiety. I lifted one little shoe out and sat down with it in my hand, gazing at its delicate, perfect shape, my heart beating quickly and the blood mounting joyously to my brain.

What a wonderful thing it is, this life in youth when

even the sight of a girl's shoe can bring one such keen, passionate pleasure!

Yet what pain, what agony it would be if by chance I had come across this shoe and held it in my hand as now, and there was no violet night to follow, no white arms going to be stretched out through its deep mauve-tinted shadows!

I was still sitting with the shoe in my hand when Viola reappeared, her arms full of lilac.

"I went down to the garden to get some of this," she said. "It looked so lovely. What are you doing, Trevor, sitting there? The woman has made the tea, and it will be much too strong if you don't come down."

She came up behind me and I saw her flush and smile in the glass as she caught sight of her shoe. I looked up, and she coloured still more at my glance.

"I am thinking about this and other things," I said smiling up at her.

She bent over and kissed me and took the shoe out of my hand.

"I am glad you like my little shoe," she said gently with a tender edge to her tone, replacing the shoe in the drawer.

"Now do come down."

She put all the lilac in a great mass in the jug and basin, and we went downstairs.

After tea we went out to explore our new and temporarily acquired territory, and found there was another flower garden at the side of the house. This, like the one in front, was hedged round with lilac laden with glorious blossom of all shades, from deepest purple through all the degrees of mauve to white. Every here and there the line was broken by a May-tree just bursting into bloom that thrust its pink or white buds through the lilac. A narrow path paved with large, uneven, moss-covered stone flags led down the centre and on through a little wicket gate into the kitchen garden beyond, so that altogether there was quite an extensive walk through the three gardens, all flower-lined and sweetly fragrant. We passed slowly along the path down to the extreme end of the kitchen garden where there was a seat under a broad-leaved fig-tree. By the side of the seat stood an old pump, handle and spout shaded by a vine that half trained and half of its own will trailed and gambolled up the old red brick garden wall. A flycatcher perched on the pump handle and thrilled out its gay irresponsible song.

"I have just come over the sea and I am so glad to be here, so glad, so glad," it seemed to be saying, and two swallows skimmed backwards and forwards low down to the earth, gathering mud from a little pool by the pump.

We sat down on the bench and looked out from under the fig-tree at the pure tranquil sky, full of gold light and just tinted with the first rosy flush of evening.

There was complete silence save for the clear, gay, rippling song of the bird, and the deep peace of the scene seemed to fall upon us like an enchanted spell.

Viola dropped her head on my shoulder with a sigh of contentment.

"I am so happy, so content. I feel as glad as that little flycatcher. It has escaped from the sea and the storms and winds, and I've got away from London, its tiresome dinners and hot rooms and all the stupid men who want to marry one."

I laughed and watched her face as it lay against me, and I saw her eyes half-closed as she gazed dreaming into the sunshine.

Faint pink clouds sailed across the sky at intervals like downy feathers blown before a breeze; the flycatcher continued its chattering song to us, some bees hummed with a warm summer-like sound over the wall.

An hour slipped by and seemed only like one golden moment. We heard a bell jangle from the direction of the house, and when I looked at my watch I saw it was time to dress for dinner.

When we retraced our steps the whole garden was bathed in rosy light and the lilac stood out in it curiously and poured forth a wonderful, heavy fragrance as we passed.

The voice of spring, that beautiful low whisper with its promise of summer and cloudless days was in all the air. Had we been married several years I do not think either Viola or I would have found Mrs. Jevons's cooking good nor praised the dinner that night; the attendance also might have been condemned. But as it was we were in that magic mirage of first days together and everything seemed perfect.

When it was over we sought the outside again and sat watching the now paling rose of the sky being replaced by clear, tender green. A passion and rapture of song, the last evening song of the birds, was being poured out on the still dewy air all round us. One by one the songsters grew tired and ceased as a pale star grew visible here and there in the transparent sky, and complete silence fell on the garden. Only a bat flitted across it silently now and then, and the white night-moths came and played by us. I had my arm round her waist and I drew her close to me and looked down upon her through the dusky twilight.

"Let us go, too, dearest, it is quite late."

She looked up, the colour waving all over her face, and smiled back at me, and we went in and upstairs.

When we reached our room, the window was wide

open as we had left it and the room seemed full of soft violet gloom, heavy with fragrance of the lilac that shewed its pale mauve stars through the shadows.

It was so beautiful, the effect of the deep summer twilight, that I told her not to light the candles.

"Shew yourself to me in this wonderful mysterious half-light, nothing can be more beautiful."

I sat down on the foot of the bed watching her, my heart beating, every pulse within me throbbing with delight.

Viola did not answer. She did not light the candles, but with the rustle of falling silk and lace began her undressing.

That night I could not sleep. The window stood open, and the room was filled with the soft mysterious twilight of the summer night with its thousand wandering perfumes, its tiny sounds of bats and whirring wings.

The cherry bloom thrust its long, white, scented arms into the room. I lay looking towards the white square of the window wide-eyed and thinking.

A strange elation possessed my brain. I felt happy with a clear consciousness of feeling happy. One can be happy unconsciously or consciously.

The first state is like the sensation one has when lying in hot water: one is warm, but one hardly knows it, so accustomed to the embrace of the water has the body become.

The other state of conscious happiness is like that of first entering the bath, when the skin is violently, keenly alive to the heat of the water.

Viola lay beside me motionless, wrapped in a soundless sleep like the sleep of exhaustion. Not the faintest sound of breathing came from her closed lips.

The room was so light I could distinctly see the pale circle of her face and all the undulating lines of her fair hair beside me on the pillow.

I felt the strange delight of ownership borne in upon me as it had never been yet.

We had not dared to pass a night together at the studio.

We had only had short afternoons and evenings, hours snatched here and there, over-clouded by fears of hearing a knock at the door, a footstep outside.

But this deep solitude, these hours of the night when she *slept* beside me, all powers, all the armour of our intelligence that we wear in our waking moments, laid aside, seemed to give her to me more completely than she had ever given herself before.

And gazing upon her in serene unconsciousness, I felt the intense joy of possession, a sort of madness of satisfaction vibrating through me, stamping that hour on my memory for ever.

The next morning we came down late and enjoyed everything with that keen poignant sense of pleasure that novelty alone can give. To us coming from a stay of months in town the small sitting-room, the open casement window, the simple breakfast-table, the loud noise of birds' voices without, the green glow of the garden seemed delightful, almost wonderful.

So curtains were really white! how strange it seemed. In town they are always grey or brown, and the air was light and thin with a sweet scent, and the sky was blue! ! !

It was a fine day, the sun poured down riotously through the snow-white bloom of the cherry-tree, two cuckoos were calling to each other from opposite sides of the wood, and their note, so soft in the distance, so powerful when near, resounded through the shining air till it seemed full of the sound of a great clanging bell, musical and beautiful.

Viola was delighted; her keen ear enjoyed the unusual sound.

"Oh, Trevor, that repeated note, how glorious it is! It reminds me of a sustained note in Wagner's *Festpiel*. I do wish they'd go on."

She seated herself by the window listening with rapture in her eyes. The woman of the house brought in our coffee, but I doubt if we should have got any breakfast, only the cuckoos wanted theirs and fortunately flew off to get it.

When the glorious musical bell rang out far on the

other side of the wood, dimmed by distance, Viola came reluctantly to the table.

"How delicious this is! this being in the country *just at first*. Look at the table with its jonquils! isn't it pretty? Look at the honey and cream!"

"I think you had better eat some of it," I answered; "or at least pour out the coffee."

Viola laughed and did so, and we breakfasted joyously, full of the curious gayety that belongs to novelty alone.

Then we went out, and the outside was equally entrancing. The scent of the lilac seemed to hang like a canopy in the air under which we walked. There was a fat thrush on the lawn, young and tailless. The sight of him and the dappled marks on his white breast gave me a strange pleasure.

We sat down on the turf finally where the cherry-tree cast a light shade, a sort of white shadow in the sunlight, from its blossoms. Viola thrust her hands down into the cool, green grass.

"How lovely this is," she said, looking up the tall tree above us. "Look at its great tent of white blossoms against the blue sky; it's like a picture of Japan!"

After a time, when we were tired of the garden, we went out and turned down the white road to explore the country.

It was very hot, and the glare from the road excessive,

but as it was all new to us it all seemed delightful, even to the white dust that coated our lips and got into our eyes whenever the breeze stirred.

After about a mile and a half of walking we came to an oak wood. The road dipped suddenly between cool, green, mossy banks and lay in deep, grateful shade from the arching oaks above. I climbed the bank on one side and looked into the wood. It was very thick and wild, apparently rarely penetrated. Through the close-growing stems of the undergrowth I saw a bluebell carpet lying like inverted sky beneath the oaks.

"The wood looks very attractive," I said as I rejoined Viola; "but we can't stay to go into it now. We haven't the time; it's half past twelve already."

"I'm sorry," said Viola, looking wistfully at the green wood. "This is the nicest part; but I suppose we can't disappoint that woman by not getting back to luncheon."

So we walked back slowly through the noonday sun, admiring the double pink May peeping out from the green hedges.

When we came in just before lunch, she took the easy chair facing the window, and I sat down on one opposite and watched her. She was wearing a white cambric dress that looked very simple and girlish; she was smiling, and her face was delicately rose-coloured after the walk.

A sense of responsibility came over me. She was my cousin, my own blood relation. I must protect her, must think for her if she would not think for herself.

"You know it's risky being down here like this. You had much better come to some rustic church with me in another village and marry me there."

"No. You know perfectly well I am not going to marry you," she said softly, looking up at me with a smile in her eyes, great pools of blue beneath their exquisitely arched lids.

"It is ridiculous to suppose that you, an artist of twenty-eight, will want to keep faithful to one woman all the rest of your life—or her life. It would be very bad for you, if you did. One can't go against Nature, and Nature has not arranged things that way. Marriage is a pleasure perhaps; but Nature never arranged marriage, and a man should not allow himself unnatural pleasures."

She was really laughing now, but I knew her resolve was perfectly serious and I did not see how I could break it up.

"Well, but some men do keep to one woman all their life and are none the worse for it; look at a country clergyman for instance."

Viola raised her eyebrows with a laugh.

"How can you be sure of the country clergyman? I expect he goes up to town sometimes. . . . However, of course I admit he is fairly faithful, but how about being none the worse for it? A country clergyman is about the most undeveloped creature you could have, and a great artist is the most developed, the nearest approach to a god of all human beings."

I did not answer, but sat silent staring at her. She looked such a sweet little Saxon schoolgirl in her white dress, but with such tremendous character and power in those great shining eyes.

"But if we marry now," I said at last, "and anything should . . . should come between us, I don't see it would be any worse than . . ."

"Than if we were living together without marriage," she put in quickly. "Yes, I think it would. Look here, if we marry now with a great blaze and fuss, and invite all our friends to see the event, which is great nonsense anyway, and then you see some other woman later you covet, it seems to me there are only three ways open to us: either you go without the woman and suffer very much in consequence and always owe me a grudge for standing in your way; or you take her and I have to profess to see nothing and look on quietly, which I could never stand, it would send me mad; or we must have all the trouble and worry and scandal of a divorce and call in the public to witness our quarrel; and why *should* we have the public to interfere in our affairs?" she added, her eyes flashing. "What is it to them whom I love or whom I live with, whom I leave or quarrel with? These are all private matters."

"And if we live together and the same thing happens?" I pursued quietly.

"Why, then we should separate, only without any trouble, any publicity; we should fall apart naturally. If you preferred any one else, you must go to her; I should slip away out of your life, and we should each be free and untied."

"If it's so much better for the man to change," I said smiling, "it must be the same for the woman."

"So it is," rejoined Viola quickly; "the more men a woman has the more developed she is, the better for her morally, if there is no conventional disgrace attaching to it. Amongst the Greeks, Aspasia and all those women of her class were far more intellectual, more developed than the wives who were kept at home to spin and rear children.

"All these things ought to be optional. If a woman loves one man so much she wants to stay with him for ever and ever, probably through such a great passion she reaches her highest development; but until she has found that man she ought to be allowed to go from one to another without any disgrace attaching to it. And, of course, just the same law holds good for the man.

"Outsiders like the world and the law ought never

to be allowed to interfere between a man and a woman. They never can know the right or the wrong of their relations to each other well enough to enable them to be judges. Nobody ever knows but the man and the woman themselves, and they ought to be left alone; what they do, whether in quarrelling or love, ought to be as private as the prayers one sends to Heaven."

She paused, and through the window came the gay, loud, triumphant call of the cuckoo seeking its mate of an hour in the heart of the glad green wood.

Viola listened with a look of delight.

"How happy they are!" she said. And the note came again, instinct with love and joy.

"How well Nature arranged everything, and how Man has spoiled it all! Fancy passion, the most subtle, evanescent, delicate, elusive emotion—and yet one so strong—fancy that being bound down by crabbed and crooked laws, being confined by wretched little conventions!"

"But, anyway, we shall have to say we are married here."

"Oh, say anything you like," rejoined Viola laughing; "saying doesn't do any harm."

"Yes, but then we must fix some place where we've *been* married and all that, do you see; we'd better go somewhere further off I think and stay away some time and come back married. I do feel very worried about it, Viola. I think it would be much simpler to do it than to lie about it."

Viola jumped up and came over to me.

"Dear Trevor, I am *so* sorry you are worried, but really it will work out all right. We will go abroad somewhere from here, we might go to Rome, it's a lovely time of year, and then to Sicily, to Taormina, . . . and we'll stay away a year and you finish the picture and I'll write an opera, and then we'll come back married to town in the season and we'll have *been* married before we leave England of course, and then it will be a year ago, and I don't think anybody will bother about it much."

I looked down upon her. She was so pretty and so dear to me: I must keep her, and if those were the only terms upon which she would stay with me I must accept them.

The landlady came into the room at this minute followed by the maid to lay the luncheon; in the land-lady's hand was a fat, black book which she presented diffidently to Viola.

"It's the Visitors' book, ma'am," she said. "I thought you and the gentleman would like to write your names in it in case of any letters . . ."

"Yes, very much," returned Viola promptly, with a little side smile at me, and sat down and wrote in it.

When she had done so, she closed the book, and as

the maid was in and out of the room during luncheon, it was not till it was finished and cleared away and we were alone that I asked her what she had written.

"Mr. and Mrs. Lonsdale; that's right, isn't it? I did not put Trevor for I always think 'make your lies short' is a good rule."

"I thought you were such a truthful person," I said a little sadly.

"So I am—to you, for instance, so I should be to any one who has the right to hear truth; but the world has no right, and I don't care what lies I tell it, it's such an inquisitive old bore!"

I laughed. Viola always made you laugh when you felt you ought to be angry with her.

"Come out now," I said, "let's enjoy this lovely afternoon. I should like to paint you under that tree," I added musingly, looking out on the tree in its white glory.

"In your usual style?" she returned laughing. "I don't think you could here. Mrs. Jevons would turn me out as not being respectable; not even being Mrs. Lonsdale would save me."

"You would make a lovely picture, even dressed," I returned, musing; "but then of course it would not sell for half the price.

"Nothing is really snapped at but the nude. That lovely landscape I painted when I was young and foolish,—it took me two years to work it off, and the veriest little daub of an unclothed girl goes directly at a hundred guineas."

"A great compliment to our natural charms," laughed Viola. "I am delighted personally at anything that is a note of protest against the tyranny of the dressmaker and fashion."

"What shall we do?" I queried; "it's beautifully hot," I added persuasively.

"I'll tell you: we will go into the oak wood; the oaks grow low and the ground and the land rise all round, no one can possibly see us without coming quite close; on that blue carpet you shall paint me lying asleep, we will call the picture 'The Soul of the Wood,' and you shall sell it for a thousand. Come along."

So it was decided, and with one of her thick cloaks, that she could throw round her instantly if surprised, and my artist's pack we started for the wood.

It was a hot golden day, the one day we should get of really fine weather in the whole English year, and when we reached the wood the light under the oak boughs was magnificent, a soft mellow glory falling down on the blue hyacinths which grew so closely together that it was as if a sea of vivid colour had invaded the dell or a great patch of the blue sky had fallen there.

We had difficulty in getting into the wood as the undergrowth of young oak scrub made it almost impenetrable; it stood up straight, and the great, swaying, huge, spreading boughs of the old oaks above came down and rested on and amongst the young oaks, like a roof upon pillars, and the leaves of both intermingled till they were like green silk curtains hung from ceiling to floor. When we had finally pushed through almost on our hands and knees to the centre of the wood, the scrub grew less close, the carpet of blue was perfect, a circle of green shut us in, we were in a magic chamber, through the roof of which came floods of green and golden light.

Viola cast aside the "tyranny of the dressmaker" and shook out her light hair. Then she threw herself on the hyacinth bed, looking upwards to the low arching roof. At that moment the call of the cuckoo, wild, entrancing, came overhead, and she raised her arms with a look of rapture as the slim grey bird dashed through the upper oak branches in pursuit of its mate. It was a perfect pose for the "Soul of the Wood," and I begged her to keep it while I rapidly caught the idea and sketched it in roughly in charcoal.

Those happy sunlit hours in the wood, how fast they slipped away! I was absorbed in the work and completely happy in it, and Viola I believe was equally happy in the delight she knew she was giving me.

We came back very hungry to our tea, and very

pleased with ourselves, the sketch, and our successful afternoon.

It was six o'clock, the light was mellowing, and a thrush singing with all its own wonderful passion and rapture on the lawn. The scent of the lilac, intensely sweet, came in at the window and filled the room.

In the evening we went out and sat under the cherry-tree, watching the stars come out and gleam through its white bloom.

"Sing me the Abendstern," murmured Viola, leaning her head against me. "I was a dutiful model all the afternoon, it's your turn to amuse me now."

So I sang the Abendstern to her under the cherry-tree, and its white shadow enveloped us both, making her face look very beautiful under it; and when I had finished singing we kissed each other and agreed that the world was a very delightful place as long as there was Wagner's music in it, and cherry-trees to sit under, and white bloom and stars and lips to kiss.

Between nine and ten, after a very countrified supper we went up to bed in the slanting-roofed room under the thatch, full still of the tender light of a spring evening.

The next day was delicious, too, and the next, but on the fourth we were quite ready to go. We had drained the cup of joy which that particular place held for us and it had no more to offer. The cherry-tree pleased us still, but it did not give us the ecstatic thrill of the first view of it. The lilac scent streamed in, but it did not go to the head and intoxicate us as when we came straight from the air of Waterloo; the thrush gurgled as passionately on the deep green lawn, but the gurgle did not stir the blood. All was the same, only the strange spell of novelty was gone.

Viola seemed so pleased to be leaving it quite hurt me. When I went upstairs I found her packing her little handbag with alacrity and singing.

"Are you glad to be going?" I asked.

"Yes," she said surprised; "are not you?"

"But you have been happy here?" I said with a tone of remonstrance.

"Oh, yes!" she exclaimed; "wildly, intensely happy! It's been four days' enchantment, but then it's gone now; we can't get any *more* out of this place. We have enjoyed it so much we have drained it, exhausted it; like the bees, we must move on to a fresh flower."

It was true that was all we could do, yet I looked round the bare attic-like room with regret. Could ever another give me more than that had done? Could there ever be a keener joy, a deeper delight than I had known in the shadows of that first violet night?

PART THREE

THE BLACK NIGHT

CHAPTER VI

IN MAYFAIR

THE spring of the next year found us installed in a small house in Mayfair, for the season.

For a year we had been abroad; the summer in Italy, the winter in Egypt, and had come back with our eyes full of colour, armed against the deadly greyness of England for three months at least.

We had travelled as Mr. and Mrs. Lonsdale, we came back as Mr. and Mrs. Lonsdale. There had been no difficulty so far. Every one seemed satisfied, and what was far more important, so were we.

The whole top floor of the Mayfair house was my studio, and made a fairly large and convenient one. We kept on the old studio as a matter of sentiment, but rarely went there now.

The "Phryne" and the Soul of the Wood" had been finished and accepted for exhibition. Both were sold, the "Phryne" for five thousand pounds, the "Soul of the Wood" for four thousand, and I had brought from abroad many unfinished sketches and partly finished pictures.

In all this time we had lived very close to each other: Viola had been my only model against an ever-varied background. Not the faintest shadow had flecked the sunshine of our passion for each other. Viola had written her operetta, and it had been taken for a London theatre. A Captain Lawton had written the libretto under the title of the "Lily of Canton." The music was weird and charming, suited to the strange Chinese story and scenery. It was to be produced in May, and Viola always spoke of the first night with excited joy.

It had been a full, rich year. Like bees, as Viola had said, we had gone from flower to flower, draining the honey from each new blossom and passing on. New places, new skies, new scenes had all in turn contributed to our pleasure and given us inspiration which took form again in our art.

The vivid desert backgrounds, the light-filled skies of Upper Egypt crept into my pictures, the cry of impassioned Eastern music in the forbidden dancing-dens of Keneh stole into Viola's refrains.

On that sunny afternoon in April, as we took tea in our tiny and gimcrack drawing-room together, Viola and I felt in the best of spirits.

"Captain Lawton and Mr. and Mrs. Dixon are coming in to dinner to-night," Viola remarked. "Lawton tells me he saw the manager yesterday, and the piece seems getting on all right."

"I am very glad," I answered. "Do you know, Viola, a Roman girl called here this morning, and wanted me to take her on as a model. She's very good. I think I'd better secure her, if . . . if . . ."

"If what . . .?" asked Viola smiling.

"Well, if you don't mind," I answered, colouring.

"Mind? I? No, dearest Trevor. Of course not. You must want a new model by now. Do engage her by all means. Is she good altogether?"

"I don't know. I have only seen her face yet. That's very lovely. Veronica she calls herself. I thought, anyway, she would do splendidly for the head."

"What a piece of good luck she should come now. You were just wanting a model for your Roman Forum picture," returned Viola. And then the matter dropped, for some women came in to tea and broke off the conversation.

At eleven o'clock the next morning I was in my studio, awaiting Veronica. I was pleased, interested, elated. The girl was really beautiful, and the sight of beauty exhilarates and animates like wine.

She was very punctual and came confidently into the room as the clock struck. The cold morning light through a north window fell upon her and instead of the light warming the face as so often happens, her face seemed to warm the light. She was about sixteen, with a skin of velvet, dark, quite dark, but clear as wine, and with a wonderful red flush glowing through the cheek; the eyes were brilliant, brown to blackness, but full of fire and lustre; her hair, dark as midnight, clustered and fell about her face in soft curls. The nose was dainty, refined, with perfect nostrils, the mouth deepest red and curved with the most tender, seducing lines. I had never seen such a face. The beauty of it was glorious, to an artist awe-inspiring.

I stood gazing at her, delighted, spellbound, and the young person keenly observed my admiration. She smiled, revealing true Italian teeth, exquisite, white, and perfect.

"I am Veronica Bernandini," she said. "I have two hours to spare in the morning and three in the afternoon."

My first thought was not to let any other artist have her; not till I had painted her at any rate and startled London with her face.

"Are you sitting to any one else?" I asked mechanically.

"No. I give the rest of my time to my family. We are very poor. My mother and father are old. I am their sole support."

I waved my hand impatiently. All models tell you that. One gets so tired of it.

"What do you want an hour? I will take all your time. You must not sit to any one else."

Her eyes gleamed, and the lovely crimson mouth pouted.

"Five shillings an hour if you take the five hours a day," she answered.

"I suppose you know that's double the ordinary price?" I said smiling. "However, I don't mind. I'll pay you if I find you sit well. Take off your hat now and sit down—anywhere. I want just to make a rough sketch of your head."

She obeyed, and I drew out some large paper sheets and found a piece of charcoal. Sitting down opposite her, I gazed at her meditatively. Now that her hat had been removed I could see the extraordinary wealth and beauty of her hair. It was black with lights of red and gold fire in it, and fell in its own natural waves and curls and clusters all about her small head and smooth white forehead.

What about a Bacchante? She was a perfect study for that. I always imagined—perhaps from seeing antiques, where it is so represented, that the head of a Bacchante should have hair like this; and it is rare enough in English models. Suppose I made a large picture—The Death of Pentheus—the king in Euripides' tragedy of the Bacchæ who in his efforts to put down the Bacchanalia was slain by the enraged Bacchantes. Suppose I put this one in the foreground. . . . But then it seemed a pity to spoil such a lovely face with a look of rage. . . . Well, anyway, let me have a sketch first, and see what inspiration came to me. I got up and looked amongst my odd possessions for a vine-leaf wreath I had. When I found it and some ivy leaves, I came back to her and fastened them round her head, in and out of those wonderful vine-like tendrils of hair. She sat demurely enough and very still while I did so, but when I wanted to unfasten the ugly modern bodice and turn it down from her throat so as to get the head well poised and free, she pressed her lips on my hand as it passed round her neck.

I drew my hand away.

"Don't be silly, or I shan't employ you," I said with some annoyance.

She pushed out her crimson lips.

"You are too handsome to be an artist; they are mostly such guys."

"Hush, be quiet now, be still," I said, moving back from her to see if I had the effect I wanted. I felt with a sudden rush of delight I had. The face was just perfect now: the head a little inclined, the leaves in the glossy hair, no more exact image of the idea the word Bacchante always formed in my mind could be imagined.

I sketched her head in rapidly. I made two or three draughts of it in charcoal, then I got my colours and did a rough study of it in colour. Her neck, like that of almost all Italians, was a shade too short, but round and lovely in shape and colour. The time passed unnoticed, and it was only when the luncheon gong sounded I realised how long I had been at work.

I sprang up and gathered the sheets of paper together.

"That's all now," I said. "I'll take you again three to six. Are you tired?" I added, as she got up rather slowly and took up her hat.

"No," she answered, shaking her head. "All that was sitting down; that's easy."

Her voice sounded flat, but I was too hurried to take much notice of it. I wanted to get down to show Viola the work.

"Well, three o'clock then," I repeated, and ran downstairs.

Viola was waiting in the dining-room, but not at the table. I went over to the window where she was standing, and showed her the sketches.

"Oh, Trevor, how lovely; how perfectly beautiful!" she exclaimed, gazing at the charcoal head.

"You have done that well, and what a glorious face!"

I flushed with pleasure.

"I'm so glad you like it. Come up this afternoon and see the model, see me work. Say you're out, and let's have tea in the studio."

"Very well," she answered as the luncheon came in; "I'll say we want tea up there. What a good idea to make her a Bacchante; it's the very face for it."

"Suppose I took her as a Bacchante dancing, the whole figure I mean, nude, under a canopy of vine leaves, make all the background, everything, green vines with clusters of purple grapes, and then have her dancing down the sort of avenue towards the foreground, with the light pouring down through the leaves. How do you think that would be?"

"I should think it would be lovely," Viola answered slowly, with a little sigh.

I looked across at her quickly.

"You would like to be my only model for the body?" I said gently, keeping my eyes on her face.

"No, Trevor, I really don't want to be selfish, and I do think you should have another, only . . ."

"Yes, only . . . ?"

"Well, when a woman is in love she does so long to be able to assume all sorts of different forms, to be different women, so as to always please and amuse and satisfy the man she loves. How delightful it would be if one could change! One can be pretty, one can be amiable, clever, charming, anything, but one cannot be different from oneself; one must be the same, one can't get away from that."

I laughed.

"I don't want you to be different. I should be overwhelmed if you suddenly changed into some one else! And whatever models I have, you will always be the best. There could not be another such perfect figure as yours."

Viola smiled, but an absent look came into her face.

After luncheon we both went up to the studio together, and Viola was ensconced in my armchair when Veronica's knock came on the door.

I said, "Come in," and she entered with the confident air of the morning. Directly she saw Viola, however, she seemed to stiffen with resentment, and stood still by the door.

"Come in," I repeated, "and shut the door."

Viola looked at her kindly and laid down the charcoal sketch in her lap.

"I have been looking at your head here and thinking it so beautiful," she said gently.

Veronica only stared at her a little ungraciously in return, and took off her hat in silence.

I put her back into position, re-arranged the fillet on her head, and set to work to complete the colour study.

We worked in unbroken silence till tea was brought up at four. Viola rose to make it, and I told the girl to get up and move about if she liked, and I set the canvas aside to dry. Viola offered the girl a cup of tea, but she refused it and went and sat under the window on an old couch, leaving us by the table.

The canvas was a success in a way so far, but the

great sweetness of the expression in the charcoal sketch of the morning was not there.

When tea was over I went up to Veronica and told her I must leave the canvas of the head to dry, I could not work more on it then, and asked her if she would pose for me as the Bacchante dancing. I wanted to see if she would do for a larger picture.

I got no answer for a minute. Veronica looked down and began to pull at the faded fringe of an old cushion.

At last I repeated my question.

"Not while *she's* here," she muttered in a low, fierce tone.

I was surprised at the resentment in look and voice.

"Nonsense," I said with some annoyance. "You can pose before her as well as before me."

Veronica did not answer, only pulled in sullen silence at the cushion.

"You are wasting my time," I said impatiently.

Veronica looked through the window.

"I shan't take off my clothes before her," she muttered defiantly.

I turned away from her in annoyance and approached Viola who had not moved from her chair on the other side of the room. She sprang up and came to meet me.

"She objects to my being here?" she said quickly. "Is it bothering you? Because, if it is, I'll go; that'll settle it."

"It's awfully stupid. I'm so sorry, Viola; it's so idiotic of her."

Viola smiled brightly up at me.

"Never mind, I'll go. You'll be down soon, now."

I held the door open for her, and with a smiling nod at me she passed through and went down the stairs. I waited till her bright head had disappeared, and then closed the door and went back to Veronica.

"Now," I said, "Mrs. Lonsdale has left us. Will you get up and stand as I want you to? Or do you want me to dismiss you?"

I felt extremely angry and annoyed. My heart beat violently. Viola had come there by my invitation, she had deprived herself of any possible society for the afternoon, and now had been practically turned out by this impertinent little model.

Veronica got sulkily up from the couch and began to undress in silence.

I walked away and flung myself into the armchair Viola had vacated, and picked up the charcoal sketch.

How sweet the face was in that! And yet what an awful little devil the girl on the couch had looked.

I was so accustomed to Viola's unfailing either good temper or self-command, that I was beginning to forget women had bad tempers as well as men.

After a minute or two Veronica came over to me; she had let her hair down, and it fell prettily on her shoulders. I laid down the charcoal sketches and looked at her critically as she approached.

Her figure had all the beauty of great plumpness and youthfulness. Every contour was round and full, and yet firm. Her body was beautiful in the sense that all healthy, sound, young, well-formed things are, but there was, as it were, no soul in the beauty, nothing transcendent in any of the lines or in the colour. It was something essentially of earth, un-dreamlike, appealing to the senses, and to them alone.

I was struck with the great contrast it presented to the form of Viola, which was so wonderfully ethereal, so divine in colour and design. Every line in it was long and tapering, never coming to a sudden stop, but merging with infinite grace into the next, and the dazzling, immaculate whiteness of it all made it seem like something of heaven. It suggested the vision, the ideal, all that man longs after with his soul, that stirs the celestial fires within his brain, not merely the flame of the senses.

In the form before me, the lines were short and often abrupt, the curves quick and expressionless; it would do capitally for the "Bacchante," it would not have served for a moment for the "Soul of the Wood."

The girl was smiling now, and appeared quite amiable. Most people are when they have got their own way. She asked me if I thought she would do.

"Yes, I think you will. Stand back there, please, against that green curtain. Now put one foot forward as if you were advancing. Yes, that's right; lift both your arms up over your head."

I got up to give her a hoop of wire to hold as an arch over her, and put a spray of artificial ivy over it.

"That'll do. Now stand still, and let's see how that works out."

The girl posed well. Evidently she was a model of considerable practice, and I obtained an excellent sketch before a quarter to six, when she said she must leave off and dress.

She did so in silence, while I studied my own work. When she had her hat on I looked up and asked her if she wanted to be paid.

"No," she answered, "we'll leave it till the end of the week. Good-bye."

"Good-bye," I said, and she went out. I laid the sketch on the table beside me, and sat thinking. A sudden blankness fell upon me as I stood mentally opposite this new idea that had never presented itself to me in the same form before, that in my former easy, wandering existence I had always welcomed a beautiful model, not only for the gain to my art, but because of the incidental pleasure it might bring me. But now I realised suddenly that this girl's beauty brought me no elation. *It was not any use,* and in a flash I saw, too, that no woman now, no beauty could be any use to me ever any more, for I was not a single irresponsible existence any longer, but involved with another which was sacred to me.

How often in the past, when entangled in some light *liaison*, I had wished for deeper, stronger emotions, something to wake the mind and stir the soul! Then in my love for Viola I had found all these and welcomed them madly. She had stirred my whole sleeping being into flame, and given me those keener and stronger desires of the brain, and satisfied them; and till now it had seemed to me that this passion for her was a free gift from the hands of Fate. Now, suddenly, I saw that the gift had its price. That, after all, there was something to be said for those light free loves of the past. That some joy had been taken out of life, now those glittering trifles, toys of the senses, were taken from me, made impossible.

For the first time I realised that a great passion has its yoke, and that, in return for the great joy it gives, it demands and takes one's freedom.

I sat motionless, feeling overwhelmed by the sudden blaze of light that the simple incident of this model's advent had thrown on an obscure psychological fact.

I saw now that my love for Viola was not wholly a gain, not something extra added to my life's-cup that made it full to overflowing, but, as always in this life, something had been taken away as well as added.

I felt as a child might feel who was presented with a magnificent gift with which he was overjoyed, but who on taking it to the nursery to add to his other treasures, saw his nurse locking these all away from him for ever in a glass case above his reach.

As the child might, I hugged my new gift to me and delighted in it, but I could not help feeling regret for those other small, glittering toys with which I had formerly played so much, now shut away behind the deadly glass pane of conscience.

It was not that Veronica appealed to me specially. I did not feel I cared whether she came to the studio again or not except for the picture, but the great principle involved, now that I was face to face with it, appalled me.

Viola had sought to leave me free, by refusing marriage with me; but, after all, what difference does the mere nominal tie make?

The essential attribute of a great passion—something that cannot be eliminated from it—is the chain of fidelity it forges round its prisoners.

I do not know how long I sat there, but at last I rose mechanically, put the sheets of paper together, and went downstairs.

As I came to the drawing-room door I heard that

Viola was playing. The door stood ajar, and silently I entered and took my seat behind her. She was improvising, just playing as the inspiration came to her, and wholly absorbed and unconscious of my presence. There was a great glass facing her, in which her whole image was reflected, and had she glanced into it she must have seen me; but she did not. Her eyes gazed out before her, wrapt, delighted; her face was quite white, her lips parted in a little smile.

I saw she was under the influence of her music and absolutely happy, full of joy, such as I could never give her. A great jealousy ran through me, kindling all that passion I had for her. The thoughts and reflections of an hour back seemed swept out of mind like dead leaves before a storm. No other lighter loves could give me one-tenth of the emotion that the pursuit and conquest of this strange soul could do. For I had not conquered it. It was absorbed in, and lived in mysteries of joy that its art alone could give it, and I was outside —almost a stranger to it.

The thought burnt and stung me, and the fire of it wrapped round me as I sat watching her. That body, so slim, so perfect, she had given me, but I wanted more, I wanted that inner spirit to be mine, I wanted to conquer that.

I watched her in a fierce, jealous anger, almost as I

might have done seeing her caressed by another lover, she was so wonderfully happy, so independent of me, so unconscious of me; but man loves that which is above him, difficult to obtain, hard to pursue. We cannot help it. We are made to be hunters, and I felt I loved Viola then with fresh passion.

Some time or other I would succeed in breaking through that charmed circle in which she lived, in making her yield up to me the spiritual maidenhood which, as it were, was hers.

I would be first and last and everything to her, and not even her art should count beside me.

I closed my eyes and put my head back on the couch where I was sitting and gave myself up to listening to the music.

How the instrument answered her! What a divine melody rose from it, floating gently on the air like quivering wings.

Then suddenly came a storm of passion, and the room was filled with a tempest of sound, while one strong thread of melody low down in the bass ran through it all and seemed a fierce reproach of one in anguish. At last one sheet of sound seemed to sweep the piano from end to end, a cry of dismay, of pain, the woe and grief of one who sees his world shattered suddenly before his eyes; then there was silence. I sprang up and clasped her in my arms.

"Trevor," she exclaimed, like one awakening from a dream; "I had no idea you were there."

"No," I said savagely; "you were so absorbed, you never noticed me come in."

"Well, I heard the model go, and I waited and waited for you to come down; but you were so long I turned to the piano to console me."

"Which it did quite well, apparently," I answered.

A sweet, tender look came over her face, and she stretched out her arms to me.

"Nothing could wholly console me for your absence," she said; "and you know that quite well; but the music always helps me to bear it."

I drew her to me and strained her close up to me in silence, longing to conquer, to come into union with that mysterious inner something we call the Soul.

Yet in this unconquerable quality, in this pursuit of that which always escapes from our most passionate embraces, man finds an inexhaustible delight.

CHAPTER VII

FREEDOM

THE weeks slipped by, and I worked hard at the painting, while Viola gave herself up to the music and all the work that the approaching production of her opera gave her. Our evenings were always spent together. We set aside two evenings in the week for our friends, giving only small dinners of eight or ten. On the other evenings when we were not dining out ourselves we went to the opera, and supper after.

I often wondered whether there was anything or nothing in the fact that we were not married to each other, which affected our feelings and relations to each other. Does that conventional bond make some subtle difference, just by its existence; and did that account for the fact that we seemed to find a greater delight in each other's society, a greater need of each other than the average husband and wife do; or was it only because we happened to be two who had met and really loved more than most people do, and had we been married, we should have felt the same?

Certainly we were looked upon as peculiar because, being married, we were so much together.

The true explanation is perhaps that, as a rule, the people who love do not marry, and those who marry do not love.

Coming home from our supper after the opera, I felt

the same passionate delight in Viola as that first evening when I had driven her to my studio. Waking in the dawn to find her sleeping on my arm, I had the same joyous elation as I had known under the thatched roof, during our first stay together. Unfortunately, however, a great passion for one object does not necessarily exclude lesser passions, or, rather, passing fancies of the senses for other objects. It is generally supposed that it does, but my experience is rather to the contrary.

With women possibly it may do so oftener than with men, but extreme constancy, absolute exclusiveness is not the natural product of a great passion. It is a question rather of sentiment and artificial restraint.

Nature is not on the side of sentiment. She is always a prodigal, with the one great aim before her of ensuring the continuance of the race.

Consequently, when a man is already loving one object with all his force, it is not Nature's plan to make him turn from all others by instinct. No, she is ever ready with others, ever rather prompting him, leading him towards others, in order that, should accident or death remove his first mate, others should not be wanting, and her great scheme should not be spoiled nor interrupted.

Nature is always on a grand scale, always acting in and for the plural, never for the singular.

Does she want one oak to survive, she throws on the ground a million acorns for that purpose.

Man she has fitted to love not one, but hundreds, and our senses act automatically and are always on the side of Nature. It is the mind alone that man has taught to act against her, and that demands and gives fidelity in love.

A woman's attitude towards a second lover, when she is deeply in love with the first, is not so often "I don't want him," as "It would grieve my first lover, therefore I will not take him."

A man, when offered a second mistress, usually thinks "I will take her, but I mustn't let the first one know." In both it is the anxiety of Nature that neither should be left mateless, part of her tremendous scheme of insurance against mischance.

And all this great love and passion which I had for Viola, passion which exhausted me almost to the point sometimes of being unable to work, did not seal my senses against the beauty of Veronica—beauty I painted daily in the studio.

I used to enjoy the afternoon spent there now with a different pleasure from that of work merely. The sensuous attraction had become very great, and I was beginning to feel it was not innocent and to half-long for, half-dread an interruption, something to break through it, end it.

Veronica professed to have fallen in love with me. It is rather a trick of models to do this. They think it can do no harm, and possibly extra benefits to themselves may accrue. Perhaps she was in love with me, if a mere covetousness of the senses can be called love. This she had, and from the first she had determined to subdue me. Her ruse of the first day had succeeded. Viola had never again come to the studio while she was there, and so hour after hour we were alone together undisturbed. I kept hard at work the whole time, hardly exchanging a word with her, and would go downstairs for tea with Viola; but she employed her eyes continually to tell her story, and caught my hand and kissed it whenever she was able.

Just at first I felt only amusement and annoyance. Then gradually I used to expect the soft look to come into the beautiful eyes, the touch of the warm lips on my hand began to stir and thrill me. I felt a vague dislike and distrust of the girl mentally, I thought she was vain, selfish, mercenary, revengeful, and bad-tempered, but with all that Nature had nothing to do. Her servants, the senses, submitted to the youth and beauty of the newcomer, and that was all Nature cared about.

One afternoon she was posing as usual, and I was painting, deeply absorbed, on the picture of the "Bacchante" when her voice suddenly disturbed me.

"May I move just for a minute?"

"Certainly," I exclaimed, looking up and laying down my brush.

The girl laid down her spray of ivy-leaves, walked across the space intervening between us, and, before I was aware of her intention, threw her arms round my neck and kissed me.

The kiss seemed to burn my lips, but with the current of passion I also felt a storm of anger against her. I sprang up and seized her shoulders, pushing her away from me.

"Don't, Trevor, don't, you are hurting me; you are hurting my shoulders," she exclaimed, the tears starting to her eyes.

I took my hands from her arms, and saw my grasp had left deep marks of crimson on them.

"Go and get dressed then, and go," I said furiously; "I'm not going to paint any more." I pushed my chair away and threw the palette and brushes on to the table near.

Veronica shrank from me and turned pale. In that moment the intense beauty of the face and figure was borne in upon me, she clung as if for support to the easel with one soft hand, all the youthful body seemed to shrink together in a beautiful dismay, great tears rolled down the cheeks from the dark reproachful eyes. I saw it all for one moment, feeling the anger sinking down under that strange influence that beauty has upon us. But I would not look at her. I turned my back on her and went over to the window, hardly conscious of what I did. I stood there for a few moments; then, suddenly, there came a cry and the sound of a fall behind me. I looked round and saw her lying, a little crushed heap, by the couch where she usually dressed.

I sprang forward, full of self-reproach. How foolish I had been! So unnecessarily harsh! I went to her. In obedience to my order, she had put some of her clothes on, and now lay there senseless apparently and quite white, her arms, still bare, stretched out on the floor beside her. She looked so pretty, so small, round, and helpless, that my heart went out to her. I felt I had been such a brute. As I stooped over her to raise her I saw the great crimson bruises I had left on her arms.

I picked her up and put her on the couch. She lay there quite still, pale, her eyes closed, unconscious.

I pushed the hair off her forehead, and, dipping my handkerchief into a glass of water on the table, pressed it on to her head. I was kneeling by the couch. The sweet, little, rounded face, the soft unconscious body lay just beneath my eyes.

She opened her eyes slowly:

"Trevor, do forgive me," she whispered, and smiled

up at me just a little, opening the curved lips; "do say you forgive me, give me one kiss."

In the violent reaction of feeling, in the torrent of self-reproach for being so hard on a child like this, the senses conquered, I put my head down, and kissed her passionately, far more passionately from that great reaction of preceding anger, on her lips.

"Dear, dear little girl, are you better?"

She threw her arms round me.

"Oh, Trevor, I do love you so, I do love you, I do love you."

Full of that great delight, so transient, so baseless, so unreasoning, yet so great, which the senses give us, of that passion in which the mind has no part, that passes over us as the wind ruffles the surface of the lake without moving the depths below, I kissed her over and over again, and pressed her to me, soft shoulders and undone hair and wounded arms.

The next moment the vision of Viola came before my brain, and I rose to my feet. Veronica caught at my hand, and, raising it to her lips, kissed it in a tempest of passion. I drew it away—

"Get up and finish your dressing," I said very gently. "This sort of thing can do you no good, Veronica. It will only mean that I cannot let you come to the studio at all."

Veronica rose from the couch obediently and resumed

her dressing. She gave me somehow the impression she was satisfied at having broken down my self-control, and hoped to win me over further by extreme docility. I walked away to the window, angry with myself, and yet angry again that that anger should be necessary. I had always been so free till now, able to gratify the fancy of the moment. This need for self-restraint was new and irritating.

Veronica came up to me when she was dressed, and asked for a parting kiss. I gave it, and she went away with a demure and sad little sigh.

When I came down from the studio I went at once to our bedroom to dress. We were dining early and going out after, and I knew I had not much time. Viola was not there; she had dressed evidently and gone down. Sometimes she would be sitting in the armchair at the foot of the bed waiting for me, but to-night she had gone down.

I walked about the room, quickly collecting my evening things and thinking. Why did I, now that I had left Veronica, feel self-reproach and regret at what had passed? What was a kiss? It was ridiculous to think of it twice.

I ran downstairs and found Viola as I had expected in the drawing-room. In her white dinner-gown and with a few violet pansies at her breast, she looked, I thought, particularly charming. She smiled as I came in, but when I approached to kiss her as was usual between us after the shortest absences, she got up, almost started up and moved away from me.

"Don't kiss me! I am so afraid you will crush my flowers."

I stopped disconcerted; she coloured slightly and took a chair further from me, I flung myself into one close to me.

It was so unlike Viola to resist any advance of mine, and on such a score, that it astonished me. Often and often I had hesitated when she had been in some of her magnificent toilettes to clasp her to me for fear of disturbing the wonderful creations, and had been laughingly derided for so doing.

"Your kiss is worth a dozen dresses," she would say, and crush me to her in spite of whatever laces or jewels might lie between; and such words had been very dear to me.

This phrase now, usual with many women, unheard before from her, struck me. The blood rushed to my head for a moment as the thought came— "Could she have seen or heard in any possible way the scene in the studio?" and then I dismissed it as quite impossible. It was coincidence, merely that. She could know nothing. Then, staring away from her into the little fire, I thought suddenly—

"Is not this the most despicable, the worst part of all

infidelity, this deceit it must bring with it? The lies, either spoken or tacit, to which it gives birth?"

There were only a few moments and then the bell called us to dinner.

Viola was just as sweet and charming as usual through the meal and after, both during the theatre party to which we went, and when we were driving home together.

The next morning when we were at breakfast alone she said in a very earnest tone:

"Trevor, you will be careful about that model of yours, won't you?"

I raised my eyebrows.

"How do you mean?"

"Don't let her draw you into anything you don't really want to do. Be a little on your guard with her. You know how detestable some women can be. They try to make men compromise themselves, and then worry them afterwards."

"I should think I ought to be able to take care of myself," I replied. Of course I was annoyed, and showed it.

"Well," said Viola, getting up from the table, "it is difficult when a girl is as beautiful as that and you are shut up for hours alone with her. When do you think the picture will be finished?"

"I don't know at all," I said, feeling more and more

annoyed. "I shall probably keep her on for another after it."

This was a pure invention of my anger at the moment, for I had fully resolved last night to get rid of Veronica and as soon as possible, and never see her again; but I objected to what seemed to me interference.

Viola turned paler almost than the cloth before us.

"Do you really wish to do so?" she asked.

"Yes," I said coldly. "Have you any objection?"

"Yes, I think it would be a great pity," she replied quietly. "You will get so drawn to her, so interested in her, it will come between us."

I looked at her in amaze and anger. Was this all coincidence? It must be. How could she possibly know what had occurred?

We are nearly all of us beasts to women when they appeal to us. Had the position been reversed and had I been speaking to Viola as she was to me, she would have been all sweetness, accepting my jealous anxiety as a compliment, recognising how sure a sign of passion it is.

"All this seems very childish and silly," I answered. "Veronica is nothing to me but a model and will never be anything than that. I shall keep her as long as I want her, and dismiss her when I choose. I don't want to discuss the matter again with you."

Viola waited till I had finished speaking, then when

I ceased, she inclined her head and went out, shutting the door noiselessly behind her.

In that moment even of anger against her, a great throb of admiration beat through me. Her attitude as she waited by the door, one hand clasping the handle, her face turned towards me, was so perfect, the acquiescence so graceful and dignified; but it was only for a moment, the anger closed over the impulse of love again, and I walked up and down the room full of resentment.

"Why should one," I muttered, "just because one loves one woman, never be supposed to kiss another, why should there be all this hateful, jealous tyranny? It is better to be free, as one is as a bachelor, and do what one likes, just take everything as it comes along."

Then it recurred to me suddenly that I was not married, not tied in any way, I was free, and the remembrance came, too, why it was so—that Viola herself had refused to take my freedom from me.

"Then when I use it to amuse myself for an hour or two this is the result," I thought stormily, trying to keep angry with Viola. "It's as bad as being married."

I tried to feel Viola was quite in the wrong, a tiresome, unreasonable, jealous person; but irresistibly my thoughts modified themselves, sobered by that sudden recollection that I was not bound to her nor she to me. Perhaps I should not have to complain of her tyranny very long. Waves of memory rolled over me against my will, memories of the wonderful passion that existed between us, something that went down to the roots of my being, that shook me to the very depths, as different as the day from the night from my passing fancy for Veronica's beauty. My mind went back to the first night at the studio; I had never felt anything for any other woman that could approach my feelings for her. She was so different from all the others. I had known a good many, and they all seemed very much alike, but Viola stood alone amongst them.

After a few minutes' more reflection, I went to look for her. I thought I would try to soften the effect of my last words to her, but I could not find her, and full of a sense of dissatisfaction, I went on at last upstairs to the studio.

When Veronica came into the room I realised the full extent of my folly the previous afternoon. Hitherto her manner had been respectful and demure enough on the surface, though always with a suggestion of veiled insolent self-confidence. Now the veil was thrown off, she was assured of herself, and showed it.

She came up to me, kissed me as a matter of course, and when I barely returned the kiss, she laughed openly and said coolly.

"What's the matter, Trevor? Viola been lecturing you?"

To hear her use Viola's name seemed to freeze me.

"Be quiet," I said sharply.

The girl merely made a grimace and began to take off her hat and let down her hair.

The morning passed dully. I did not paint well. The impersonal state of mind in which alone good artistic work can be produced was not with me.

When I went down to luncheon I found Viola looking very pale and ill. This made me feel cross. Ill-health very rarely excites pity or sympathy in men, but nearly always a feeling of vexation and annoyance. "Why should she worry herself?" I asked myself angrily, "when there was nothing to worry about."

She had generally a very warm pink colour glowing in her face, which disappeared if anything worried or grieved her. It was gone now, and I knew it was my words of the morning that had driven it away.

"I looked for you this morning before I went up to paint," I said; "but couldn't find you."

"I am so sorry," she answered with a quick smile. "What did you want me for?"

"To tell you you needn't worry about Veronica. She is absolutely nothing to me."

"Then, if she is, why will you not send her away, or at least when the 'Bacchante' is finished?"

"Because I don't see any necessity," I answered.

"Besides, if I get any other model you would feel the same, wouldn't you, about her?"

"Any model you kissed and desired. Yes, certainly."

We were both standing now facing each other. Viola was deadly pale, as she always became in any conflict with me.

I stood silent for a moment.

I could not understand how she knew and could speak so definitely, but I could not lie and deny it, so I said nothing.

"Do you mean that I am never to kiss another woman as long as I live?" I asked, a shade of derision coming into my voice.

"No, only as long as we are what we are to each other."

A chill fell upon me. I could not think of a time when she would not be with me, could not face the idea of change.

The light fell across her very bright and waving hair, and caught the tips of her eyelashes and fell all round her exquisite, girlish figure, full of that wonderful grace I had never seen in any other.

"It is a pity to make your love, which otherwise would be such a divine pleasure, a thing of restraint and fetters," I said slowly.

"But it is a mutual obligation in love," she said in a very low tone. "It must be so. You would not wish

me to kiss any of the men who come here, would you?
They often ask me to."

Her words gave me suddenly such a sense of surprise
and shock, it was almost as if she had struck me in the
eyes.

"*No*," I said involuntarily, the instinct within me
speaking without thought.

"Well, that is what I say," answered Viola gently.
"A great passion has its fetters. I don't see how it can
be helped. You can have the promiscuous loves of all
the women you meet, or you can have the absolute
devotion of one; but I don't see how you can have
the two."

My heart beat, and the blood seemed going up to my
head, confusing my reason. I felt angry because I
knew she was right.

"Well, really it seems that the first might be better
if one's life is to be so limited."

Viola did not answer at all. I turned and walked
towards the window and stood looking out for a few
minutes. When I turned round the room was empty.

I went up to the studio, but again I could not paint.
The pale, unhappy face of Viola came between me and
the picture.

To Veronica I hardly spoke. Her beauty neither
attracted nor even pleased me. She was the cause
of all this vague cloud rising up in my life, which had

hitherto been intensely happy and allowed me to do the very best in my art.

Her efforts to attract me and to draw me from my work only annoyed and irritated me, and when I went down to tea I told her to go, that I should not paint afterwards.

No one happened to be calling that afternoon, so Viola and I were alone. There was hardly any constraint between us even after what had passed at luncheon. We were so much one, so intimate, mentally as well as physically, that we could not quarrel with each other any more than one can quarrel with oneself. One can be cross with oneself occasionally, but not for long.

We neither of us referred to Veronica or anything disagreeable, but gave ourselves up to the joy of each other's society. When I told her I was not going back to paint she was delighted, and we planned to dine early and go to the Empire after.

The ballet seemed to amuse her, and when we returned and went up to our room she was in the lightest and gayest of spirits. This room was the only one in the house in the furnishing of which Viola had taken the slightest interest. In all the others she had allowed things to stand just as we found them, just as our landlord had thought good to leave them, but in this one much had been added to the contents written down in the inventory and so much altered that our landlord would indeed have been astonished if he had suddenly looked in. The bed was a triumph of artistic skill, designed and arranged under her own directions, the curtains enclosing it were delicate in colouring and so soft in fabric that the bed seemed enveloped in a mass of blue clouds, gold-lined, and all the sheets and clothing were filmy and lace-edged, and must have been the despair of the steam laundry; a blue silk covering, the colour of her own eyes, and embroidered with pale pink roses, gold-centred, reposed on it, matching the curtains, and an electric lamp shaded in rose colour depended from the French crown above the head; a lamp which flooded the bed with light when all the curtains were drawn and shut out the lights of the room. The carpet was blue also, and the heavy curtains over all the windows matched it, edged with, and embroidered in gold.

The toilet-table, though simple enough in its arrangements, for Viola needed no cosmetics, no lotions, no manicure nor other evil inventions, was always a lovely object. On its pale rose covering lay her gold-backed brushes and comb, her gold hand-mirror with cupids playing on it, her little gold boxes of pins, and always vases of fresh geraniums, white and rose-pink. Out of the room at one side opened a smaller one, it was not used as a chapel nor yet as a dressing-room.

We dressed together and took pleasure in so doing, as we did in everything that threw us into intimate companionship. We had no need of dressing-rooms since there were no teeth to come in and out, no wigs to be taken off and put on, no secrets on either side to be jealously guarded from one another. No, the room opening out of ours was a supper-room, where, when we came back late from opera or theatre, we could always count on finding cold supper and champagne. I went in to-night and turned on all the lights, which were many, while Viola laid aside her dress and slipped into a dressing-gown, something as fragile and beautiful as a rose-leaf, suiting her delicate, elusive beauty. She followed me into the little supper-room, and as I turned and saw her on the threshold, the delicacy of the whole vision struck me. A pain shot into my heart suddenly. Supposing I ever lost her? Saw her fade from me?

Her eyes were wide-open and laughing, a faint colour glowed in the white transparent skin, the lips were a light scarlet, parted now from the milky teeth.

I made two steps forwards and caught her and crushed her up tightly to my breast and kissed her and made her sit on my knee while I poured out some champagne.

"Now drink that," I commanded; "you look as if you needed something material. You look like a vision that may vanish from me into thin air."

Viola laughed and drank the wine.

"Trevor," she said reflectively, as if following up some train of thought she had been pursuing already a long time. "What heaps of wonderfully beautiful girls and women we saw to-night. Wouldn't you like some of them?"

I laughed.

"Some of them! Supposing you send me up a dozen or two?"

"No, but really I was thinking as I sat there to-night, how pretty they were, and how varied. I can quite understand how a man would like to try them all."

"You would object, I am afraid," I said gravely. "You object even to Veronica."

"I know. I don't think it's possible to do otherwise. I shouldn't love you if I didn't. But if you gave me up you could have all these others."

"Well, you see, it is the other way; I have given them all up for you."

"I know, but is it wise for your own happiness? I thought about it a great deal to-night."

"Women like that can give one only the simple pleasure of the senses. It is very much the same with them all; but with you there is some extraordinary passion created in the brain as well as in the senses, that makes it a different thing."

"I am so glad," she murmured, leaning her arms on the table and looking at me with eyes absorbed and abstracted.

"There is no single thing in this world I would not do to give you pleasure, to delight and satisfy you. I have never refused you anything, have I?"

"Never."

And it was true. She never had refused me anything it was in her power to give. Still she held something that was not yet mine; the inner spirit of the Soul.

Days passed and things continued in the same way. I had not the strength of mind to dismiss Veronica, to deprive myself of that subtle, delicious pleasure that lay in her soft kisses, in the bloom of her beauty, in her professed devotion to myself. The Bacchante was not quite finished, so that gave me the outward excuse. The excuse I put forward to myself was that Viola could not possibly know what I felt for the girl nor what I did, and so it could not hurt her.

Veronica made no secret of her wishes to tie me more closely to her still. But, in spite of the clamour of the senses, there was something within me or round me that held me irresistibly from this.

All that I had done already I knew that Viola would forgive, even though it grieved and distressed her. If

I went further I did not know that she would ever forgive, and that made an insurmountable barrier that nothing Veronica could do or say could break down.

The weeks slipped by and brought us to the date when Viola's operetta was to be produced. On the evening which she had so looked forward to, now it had come, she seemed tired and spiritless, and we dressed for dinner almost in silence. Captain Lawton and another man who had helped in the production of the piece were dining with us, and we were then going on to our box at the theatre.

At dinner Viola seemed to regain some of her old gay spirits, and the light rose colour I loved crept back into her cheeks as she laughed and talked with Lawton seated on her right hand. I had always thought him a particularly handsome fellow, and to-night it struck me suddenly what an extremely attractive man he must be in a woman's eyes. He was dark and a little sunburnt from being in South Africa, and, combined with really beautiful features and a fine figure, he had that dashing grace of carriage, that unaffected simple manner of the soldier, which even by itself has a charm of its own.

I looked at Viola curiously, and wondered how she felt towards this man who was so obviously in love with her. Whether it moved her at all to see those dark eyes fill with fire as she smiled at him, to know that the whole of this engaging personality was hers if she chose to stretch out her hand and claim it.

The dinner passed off well, thanks principally to the inexhaustible tide of good spirits and fun that flowed from Lawton. We took a couple of hansoms afterwards and arrived at the theatre in good time.

The "Lily of Canton" went smoothly from beginning to end. The crowded house laughed and applauded the whole time. In fact, the humour and fun of Lawton's libretto were irresistible, and the beautiful airs that Viola's fancy had woven in and out to carry the wit of Lawton's sparkling lines enchanted the audience.

At the end there were calls for both of them to appear before the curtain, and Viola left the box with him, radiant and smiling. When they both appeared on the stage the enthusiasm was unbounded. Viola was in white, and her delicate, rose-like fairness delighted the audience, and the women clapped Lawton with good-will. Handsome, easy, dignified, graceful, and debonair as usual, he smiled and bowed his acknowledgments over and over again beside Viola, into whose face came the wrapt, glad look that her music always gave, replacing the expression of pain she had worn now for so many weeks.

I sat in our box watching her, with sore, jealous

feelings rising up like mists over the pride I had in my possession. As the whole scene and her triumph stirred and roused my passion for her, some voice seemed interrogating me—"Is she and her love not enough for you? Why do you wear thin and fray the delicious tie between you?"

They were both up again in the box beside me, directly surrounded by congratulating friends; and then Lawton gathered together his party and we all filed off in a stream of hansoms to the supper that he was giving in Viola's honour. It was already daylight before we reached home.

The next evening I had to attend an artists' dinner. It was for men only, so that Viola was not invited. I spent a very busy morning and afternoon in the studio. The Bacchante was almost finished, and I had made up my mind to dismiss Veronica as soon as I was sure I was satisfied with the picture and did not need her again. Full of this resolve, I was perhaps a little more careless than usual, less on my guard, and when at the end Veronica came to kiss me, I returned her caress with more warmth than I was accustomed to do. It did not really matter, I thought; the girl would be gone in a day or two and I should have no more to do with her.

Feeling rather pleased with myself for having taken the decided resolution to dismiss her in order to please

Viola I went downstairs, and was rather vexed when I met her to see her looking particularly white and ill. She had seemed fairly well at luncheon, and I could not shake off the extraordinary idea that my conduct with Veronica through the afternoon was in some way connected with her pallor and expression now.

I had it on my lips to say—"I have decided to dismiss the model," when that feeling of irritation against her for looking so wretched came uppermost and held the words back.

If she couldn't trust me and would worry about things when I told her not to, she might worry and I would let her alone.

It really always hurt and alarmed me so much to see Viola look ill or delicate that it made me angry with her, instead of extra considerate and kind as I should have been.

She came upstairs to be with me while I dressed, and sat in the arm-chair at the foot of the bed.

I asked her if she had a headache, and she said, "No."

"What did you do all this afternoon?" I asked. "Did any one come in to tea?"

"No, nobody came. I was lying on a sofa in the drawing-room most of the time, thinking. I didn't feel able to do anything."

I did not ask her what she had been thinking about, but went on dressing in silence.

Before I left I kissed her, but it was rather a cold kiss, as I felt she ought to be happy and pink-cheeked as a result of my good intentions—unreasonably enough, since I had not told her of them.

She accepted it, but seemed to hesitate as if she wished to say something to me. I saw her grow paler and her lips quiver. She did not speak, however, and so in rather a strained silence we parted and I went downstairs.

How I regretted that coldness afterwards! How mad and blind one is sometimes where one loves most!

I did not enjoy the dinner at all because I could not deny to myself that I had been unkind to her, with that tacit unkindness that is so keenly felt and is so difficult to meet or combat. I left the hotel where the dinner had been held quite early, and drove back to the house, longing and impatient to be with her again, hold her in my arms, and tell her all I had resolved and been thinking about, and kiss the bright colour back into her face again.

I let myself in with my latch-key and ran up the stairs into the drawing-room.

It was brightly lighted, but empty. I was just going to seek her upstairs when a note set up before the clock on the mantelpiece caught my eye.

I crossed the room, took it up, tore it open, and ran my eyes hurriedly down it, line after line.

"*Dearest,*

"Our relations have entered upon a new phase lately. I suppose it cannot be helped, it is merely the turning on of the wheel of time. We cannot stay the wheel, still less turn it back. All we can do is to adjust ourselves to the new position.

"You have wished for your freedom. It is yours. I have never wanted to take it away, but I feel I cannot go on dedicating my life and every thought I have to you as I have done, if you wish to share with others all that has been mine and all that I value most in this or any world. I have tried, but it is beyond me. You cannot think what I have suffered in these last weeks. I have reasoned with myself, asked myself what did it matter what you did when you were away from me, why should one rival now matter more than those the past has held for me? I have argued, reasoned, fought with myself, but it is useless. These unconquerable instincts of jealousy have been placed in us and are as strong as those other instincts of desire that excite them.

"The life of the last few weeks is killing me. I am losing my health, losing my power to work. It is the concentration of all my thoughts upon you that is maddening, impossible now that you no longer belong to me. Even your presence, once the sun of my existence, is painful to me now; and when you come

straight from another woman to kiss me, it is agony.
I cannot bear it.

"You thought I did not know all the kisses and
caresses you have given Veronica. Dear Trevor, a
woman always knows—perhaps a man does, too.
Certainly I knew. One does not have to see or hear;
there is a sense, not yet discovered, that is above all the
others, that tells us these things. When you came
from her to me you brought with you an influence that
killed. Perhaps it was that you were surrounded with
an electricity from her that was hostile to my own.

"I have felt lately a longing to be away from you,
a longing to escape from pain and torture, but the
music keeps me in town, and we cannot well separate
here without a scandal, which I know you would not
wish. So I am going to try and escape mentally from
you, though our bodies must occupy the same house
for a little while longer.

"I am going to try to interest myself in others,
not to think of you, not to care for you as I have done.
We have both been foolish perhaps, as you say, in limit-
ing our lives to each other, let us end the idea between
us. Let us be like ordinary married people. You
are free to choose whatever paths of pleasure open
before you, I am the same. To-night when you come
back you will find this letter instead of me. I shall
dine out with one of these men who want me and after-

wards spend the evening with him. I will come back early enough to cause no comment, but I will not come to your room, as I do not suppose you will want me. I have had another room put ready, and I shall go there.

"Good-bye, dearest one; if you could know all the agony that has gone before this breaking of the tie between us! Now I seem to feel nothing; I am dead. I can't cry; can't think any more.

"VIOLA."

I read this letter through with an agonised terror coming over me, that gripped and wrung my heart, through the cloud of amaze that filled me. Towards the end the words seemed to stab me. As I came to the conclusion the truth broke upon me in a blinding, lightning flash. *I* had lost her. But it was incredible, unthinkable. She was part of my life, part of myself. I still lived; therefore, she was mine. I felt paralysed. I could not grasp fully what she had said, what she intended me to understand. It was as when one is told a loved one is dead. It means nothing to us for a moment. Reason goes down under a flood of sickening fear. I read the last page over again.

Then I sprang to my feet and stared round the empty room as if seeking an explanation from it. It offered none. All round me was orderly, placid. Only within me burned a hell, lighted by those written words. It was very quiet, only an occasional drip of the June rain outside broke the stillness.

An exquisite picture of Viola laughed joyously back at me from a little table covered with vases of white flowers, white as she had been that first night at the studio. . . .   . . .

O God in heaven, what *had* I done to bring this ruin into my own life? *Had* I deserved it? Had I? I thought wildly.

What had I done? What did it all mean? Veronica? A few kisses? the impulse of passion? It was nothing, everything was nothing to me beside Viola. She must have known that. Then I recalled her appeals to me. She had asked me to give up Veronica, why had I not done so? Instead, how had I met Viola; how had I answered her? My own words were hurled back upon me by memory and fell upon me like blows, so had they fallen upon her. How could I have been so mad, so blind?

Her favourite chair was pushed a little from the fire; by its side I noticed something white, and stooped mechanically to pick it up. It was her handkerchief, crushed together and soaked through and through. How she must have been crying to wet it like that! At the corner it was marked with blood, as if she had pressed it to bitten lips.

My own eyes filled with scorching tears as I looked at it.

It was the one sign of the passion and agony that had raged in that room before I came back.

If I had only returned sooner! I put the handkerchief in my breast, and took up her letter again. Could I do anything, anything now to follow, to recall her?

I looked at the clock, and ice seemed to close round my heart and chill it. It was already eleven. Then the phrase about the other room struck me. Could she have possibly returned? I opened the door and went upstairs and through all the rooms in the house. All were empty. I saw the bedroom farthest from mine had been put ready for occupancy, and some few trifles of her own taken from our room and put into it. Then I came back, sick with apprehension, to the drawing-room again, questioning what I could do.

To whom would she have gone? As the thought came all the blood in my body seemed to seethe and rage, but the question had to be faced. For a moment no definite idea would form itself. Then the recollection of Lawton dashed in upon me. The man's head seemed photographed suddenly on all the pale walls round me; handsome, brilliant, engaging, well born, and well bred, he was the man of all others surely to attract her.

She would go to him, they would dine together, she

would return to his chambers with him. . . . She had not come back yet.

For a few moments I was mad. I laid my hand on the back of the chair near me, and it was smashed in my grip. Then the madness passed over, and I could think again. I went upstairs, took out my revolver, and loaded it. I thought I would go round to Lawton's place, . . . but, when coming downstairs again, the thought struck me—Suppose it was not Lawton? What would the latter think of my sudden appearance, my enquiries? Twelve had now struck.

There was just a possibility that she would not fulfil her letter, that she would come back to me; but if I by my actions to-night brought any publicity on what she had done, I should make an injury where none existed.

I thought for some time over this, and it seemed impossible for me to do anything but wait for her return— wait till I knew.

The thought of her name, her reputation, and how I might possibly injure them now held me there motionless.

It seemed incredible that she could be so long away and yet her absence mean nothing. But the other supposition, the thought of her passing from me, seemed more incredible still.

I know how great her love for me was, and love

like ours is not easily swept aside and its claims broken down. Still, in a paroxysm of jealous agony and resentment against me, all might be obscured, and if Lawton were there persuading . . .

And this, something of this pain, I now felt, she had suffered, as the soaked handkerchief told me.

How I loathed the thought of Veronica! Love, even when it has expired, leaves some tenderness of feeling to us; passion once dead leaves nothing but loathing.

I got up and wrote a few lines of dismissal. It was something to do, something to distract my devouring thoughts. I enclosed a cheque for all, and more than the sum due to her. Then I flung the letter on the table, and pushed the thought of her out of my mind.

I paced up and down the room, looking constantly at the clock. What were these fleeting moments taking from me? My brain seemed on fire and full of light. Picture after picture rose before me, vivid, brilliant— all pictures of Viola and hours passed with her. What a wonderful personality she had, and I alone had possessed it. How utterly and entirely she had given herself to me, me alone of all the many who coveted her. I had been the first, the only one for her, till my own hand had foolishly cut the ties that bound us together. If I lost her, suppose I gained everything else in the world, would it content me? Could I lose her? Could

I let her go? But I *had*. I glanced at the clock. It was now one. She had not returned. By this time she had passed from me to another. The pain, the acute pain of it, of this thought seemed to divide my brain like a two-edged sword. What had I done?

Why had I not realised that I should feel like this? To have and then to lose while one still desires, this is the most horrible pain in the world. The animals feel it to the point of madness, and they are wise, they do not court it. They will tear their rival, even the female herself, in pieces rather than yield her up. But I! What had I done? A mate had nestled to my breast, and I had not been wise enough to hold it there. And now I suffered; how I suffered! My brain seemed to writhe in those moments of agony like a body on the rack or in the flames. Each thought was a torture: sweet recollections came to me like the breath of flowers, only to turn into a fresh agony of despair.

There is no pain so absolutely black in its hideous agony as jealousy. The other mental pains of this life may last longer, but there is none that cuts down deeper, that possesses such a ravening tooth, while it lasts, as this.

The vision of Lawton's face was like a brand upon my brain. I saw it everywhere, as it had looked when she smiled upon him at dinner.

Suddenly, as I paced backwards and forwards, I heard a little noise outside, a light footfall on the stairs or landing. I stood still, my heart seeming to knock about inside my chest as if it wanted to leap out between the ribs. Then I went to the door and threw it wide open. She stood there just outside. The light from within fell upon her, and my eyes ran over her, questioning, devouring, while waves of hope and terror seemed dashing up against my brain like the surf over a rock.

She looked collected, mistress of herself, her dress and hair were perfect in arrangement as when she had started, on her face was a curious look of gladness, of relief, of decision, of triumph. What was its meaning?

I took both her hands and drew her over the threshold. She came gladly. She must have seen the agony of fear, of questioning in my face, for after a swift look up at me she said impulsively:

"I am so glad to be back with you, Trevor."

I could not answer her. I stood silent. The sick fatigue of hours of painful emotion was creeping over me, and the agony of longing to know everything from her lips seemed to paralyse me.

"I could not, after all, dearest," she said, in a very low tone. "I could not do anything on my side to sever myself from you, so I have come back to you."

Her voice seemed to come to me from a long distance, but every word was clear and distinct. The relief of the loosening of the pressure of one hideous idea was intense. I took a chair beside her and put my arm round her shoulders.

"Tell me what has happened, then, since you left me."

She was drawing off her gloves slowly; the flesh of the fingers and wrist was slightly indented from long pressure of the kid. I saw that her glove had not been removed for several hours. A great tide of pleasure and relief broke slowly over me.

"Well, I went straight from here to Lawton's chambers, and he was out; so I sat down in one of his easy chairs by the fire to wait for him. I sat and sat there, looking into the fire, and somehow I forgot all about Lawton and began thinking about you and the pictures and your wonderful voice and all the delightful times we had had together; and then I thought of all I had always tried to do for you, and how you were the first, the very first man I had ever cared for or done anything for, and how I had always belonged to you; and it seemed a pity to spoil it all—if you understand. I felt I could not with my own hands pull down the beautiful fabric of my love for you that I had built up. I felt I could not give myself to any one else, there seemed something irresistible holding me from it. You must do what you like, be faithful or not to me, but I must be faithful to you."

She threw back her head and looked at me. Her elusive loveliness, lying all in colour and bloom and light, was at its height. She was intensely excited, and the excitement paled the skin, widened the lustrous eyes, heightened the extreme delicacy of the face. I bent over her and kissed her as I had never done yet; it was one of those moments in life when the soul seems to have wings and fly upwards.

After a moment.

"And then," I said, "did you come back to me?"

"Well, gradually, as I sat there, a horror of Lawton, of everything came over me. I did not know how long I had sat there. I looked at my watch: it was two. I was terrified. I only wanted to escape. I got up to go, and just then I heard Lawton coming in. There was a screen near me, and it did just occur to me I might conceal myself and pass out as he went to the inner room; but I did not like the idea of hiding in any one's rooms, so I stood still, and he came in."

She was silent, and I felt suddenly plunged back into a mist of questioning horror. What had passed between these two? Had any links in some new chain been forged?

But she was mine! Mine! and I would never let her go.

"What did you say?" I asked her. My throat was so dry the words were hardly more than a whisper.

"He started of course on seeing me, and then rushed forwards and said, 'Darling,' or something of that sort. I hardly heard what he said. I said simply: 'I was just going when you came in. I can't stay.' Then, of course, he asked me why I had come and all that and, oh, heaps and heaps of things. You know all the usual things a man does say, and I answered if he really cared for me he would let me go at once. Then he walked to the door, shut and locked it, and put the key in his pocket."

She paused, and I looked away from her. I was in such a passion of rage against the man, and almost also with her for putting herself in such a position, I did not care for her to see my eyes.

"Go on," I said; "what did you do?"

"I asked him why he had locked the door, and he said to prevent my going until I had told him why I had come. I said I had changed my mind in the hours I had sat there, and he answered: 'Well, you will change it again if you stay here some more hours,' and he came and sat on the chair arm beside me. You see, Trevor, it wasn't his fault a bit, for he guessed I had come with all sorts of nice feelings for him, and he felt it was only his part, as it were, to play up to the situation, that it would be impossible to do anything but seem to wish to keep me when I had come."

"Don't trouble to tell me all that," I said angrily; "I

know what Lawton feels for you. I know he is wild about you. I wonder you are not murdered. Go on, what did he do?"

"He was awfully good and nice. He tried for an hour to persuade me. He wanted to kiss me, of course. I said I was in his power, but that he would kill me before I would kiss him voluntarily. I think that convinced him, for he walked straight to the door and unlocked it and threw it open. Then he said he couldn't let me go into the streets at that hour alone, and so he came with me. He walked all the way here and left me at this door. That's all."

There was silence. Such a tremendous upheaval of emotions and feelings seemed surging within me I could not speak. My voice seemed dried dead in my throat. No words came before my mind that I could use.

Dawn was creeping slowly into the room. The hideous black night was over. Pale light, very soft and grey, but overpowering, was stealing in, mingling with the electric gold glare it was so soon to kill. It seemed to me like that mysterious, impalpable spirit we call love that is overpowering, dominant over everything, before which the false glare of the fires of sense pale into nothingness.

"Trevor," she said at last, breaking the silence of the pale, misty room, "are you glad I decided as I did?

You must do just what you like; I only felt I could not do anything against you."

I turned and drew her wholly into my arms, and at that warm, living contact my voice came back to me.

"You are my life, my soul, and you ask if I am glad you've come back to me? There is nothing in the world for me really but you. Everything else is dust and ashes, that can be swept away by the lightest transient wind. You are the very life in my veins, and you must be mine always, as you have been from the very first."

I pressed my lips down on hers with all the force of that fury of triumph which rose within me. I did not want her answer. I merely wanted to force my words between her lips, to drive them home to her heart. She was my regained possession, and the joy of it was like madness. She put her arms round my neck and lay quite still and passive, close pressed against my heart, and our souls seemed to meet and hold communion with each other and there was no need of any more words.

PART FOUR

THE CRIMSON NIGHT

CHAPTER VIII

LOSS

WE had left town and come down to the country. Viola had not seemed quite so well in the last three months since the night of our reconciliation, and even here in the country she did not seem to regain her colour and her usual spirits.

She declared, however, there was nothing the matter with her, and we had been intensely happy.

One morning when we came down to our rather late breakfast I found a long, thin, curiously addressed letter lying by my plate.

Viola took it up laughingly, and then I saw her suddenly turn pale, and she laid it back on the table as if the touch of it hurt her.

"Oh, Trevor, that is a letter from Suzee! I am sure it is! Why should it come now, just when we are so happy?"

I looked at her in surprise, and took up the letter to cut it open.

"What makes you think it comes from her?" I asked; "it is not at all likely."

"I know it does," she said simply; "I feel it."

I laughed and opened the letter, not in the least believing she would be right. The first line, however, my eye fell upon shewed me it was from Suzee. The queer, stiff, upright characters suggested Chinese writing, and the first words could be hers alone:

"Dear Mister Treevor,

"Do you remember me? I am in awful trouble. Husband died and also baby. I sent here to be sold for slave to rich Chinaman. Please you buy me. Send my price 500 dollars to Mrs. Hackett, address as per above.

"Dear Treevor, dear Treevor, do come to me. You remember the wood?

"I am yours not sold yet,

"Suzee."

I read this through with a feeling of amaze. Suzee had for so long been a forgotten quantity to me, something left in the past of the Alaskan trip, like the stars of the North, that her memory, thrown back suddenly on me like this, startled me.

I handed the letter to Viola in silence. She read it through, and then pushed it away from her.

"I told you so. There is no peace in this world!"

"But it needn't affect us, dearest," I said. "Suzee is nothing to me now. I don't want her. There is nothing to distress you."

"But you'll have to do something about it, I suppose," returned Viola gloomily. She was making the tea, and I saw her hands shook.

"I believe you would like to go. It would be a new experience for you. You would go if that letter came to you when you were living as a bachelor, wouldn't you?"

"Possibly I might. But then, of course, when one is free it is different. Everything is different."

"Free!" murmured Viola, her eyes filling. "I hate to think I am tying you."

"It is not that," I said gently; "one does not want to do the same things, nor care about them."

"You wanted Veronica and didn't have her on my account, I am not going to prevent you doing this. You must go if you want to."

She threw herself into the easy chair with her handkerchief pressed to her mouth. The tears welled up to her eyes and poured down her white face uncontrollably.

"Dearest, dear little girl," I said, drawing her into my arms, "you are upsetting yourself for nothing. I don't want to go, I shan't think of going. I am perfectly happy; you are everything to me."

She leant her soft head against me in silence, sobbing for some seconds.

"Come and have breakfast," I said, stroking her

hair gently, "and don't let us think anything more about it. If fifty Suzees were calling me I should not want to go."

Viola dried her eyes and came to the table in silence. We had other letters to open, and we discussed these, and no further reference was made to Suzee then.

Viola looked white and abstracted all day, but it was not till after dinner, when we were taking our coffee on the verandah, that she gave me any clew to her thoughts. Then she said suddenly:

"Trevor, I want you to let me go away from you for a year."

I gazed at her in astonishment. She looked very wretched. All the usual bright colour of her face had fled. Her eyes were large, with the pupils widely dilated in them. There was a determined, fixed expression on the pale lips that frightened me.

"Why?" I said, merely drawing my chair close to hers and putting my arm round her shoulders.

"That is just what I can't tell you," she answered. "Not now. When I come back I will tell you, but I don't want to now. But I have a good reason, one which you will understand when you know it. But do just let me go now as I wish, without questions. I have thought it over so much, and I am sure I am doing the right thing."

"You have thought it over?" I repeated in surprise. "Since when? Since this morning, do you mean?"

"No, long before that. Suzee's letter has only decided me to speak now. I have been meaning to ask you to let me go for some time, only I put it off because I thought you would dislike it so and would feel dull without me. But now, if you let me leave you, you can go to Suzee for a time, and she will amuse and occupy you, and if you want me at the end of the year I will come back."

The blood surged up to my head as I listened. How could she deliberately suggest such things?

Did she really care for me or value our love at all?

In any case, for no reason on earth would I let her go.

"No, I shall not, certainly not, consent to anything so foolish," I said coldly; "I can't think how you can suggest or think such a thing is possible."

Viola was silent for a moment. Then she said:

"When I come back I would tell you everything, and you would see I was right."

"I don't know that you ever would come back," I said, with sudden irrepressible anger.

"If you go away I might want you to stay away. You talk as if our emotions and passions were mere blocks of wood we could take up and lay down as we pleased, put away in a box for a time, and then bring them out again to play with. It's absurd. You talk of going away and driving me to another woman, and then my coming back to you, as if it was just a simple matter of our own will. Once we separate and allow our lives to become entangled with other lives we cannot say what will happen. We might never come together again."

Viola inclined her head.

"I know," she said in a low tone. "I have thought of all that. But if I stay there will be a separation all the same, and perhaps something worse."

"What do you mean by a separation?" I demanded hotly.

"Well, I cannot respond to you any more as I used. I must have rest for a time," she answered in a low tone.

I looked at her closely, and it struck me again how delicate she looked. She was thinner, too, than she had been. Her delicate, almost transparent hand shook as it rested on the chair arm.

The colour rushed burning to my face as I leant over her.

"But, darling girl, if you want more rest you have only to say so. Perhaps I have been thoughtless and selfish. If so, we must alter things. But there is no need to separate, to go away from me for that."

"No, I know," returned Viola in a very tender tone; "I should not for that alone. You are always most good. It is not that only. There are other reasons why I would rather be away from you until we can live together again as we have done."

"And you propose to go away, and suggest my living with another woman till you come back?" I said incredulously; dismay and apprehension and anger all struggling together within me for expression.

"Would it be more reasonable of me to expect to leave you and you to wait absolutely faithful to me till I came back?" she asked, looking at me with a slow, sad smile, the saddest look I had ever seen, I thought, on a woman's face. I bent forwards and seized both little hands in mine and kissed them many times over.

"Of the two I would rather you did that. Yes," I said passionately. "But there is no question of your going away; whatever happens, we'll stick to each other. If you want rest you shall have it; if you are ill I will nurse you and take care of you; but I shan't allow you to go away from me."

She put her arms round my neck. "Dear Trevor, if you would trust me just this once, and let me go, it would be so much better."

"No, I cannot consent to such an arrangement," I answered; "it's absurd. I can't think what you have in your own mind, but I know nothing would be a greater mistake than what you propose. The chances are we should never come together again."

There was silence for a moment, broken only by a heavy sigh from Viola.

"Won't you tell me everything you have in your own mind?" I said persuasively. "I thought we never made mysteries with one another; it seems to me you are acting just like a person in an old-fashioned book. You can tell me anything, say anything you like, nothing will alter my love for you, except deception—that might."

"And you seem to think separation might," returned Viola sadly.

"I don't think it's a question of separation altering my love for you, but in separation sometimes things happen which prevent a reunion."

Viola was silent.

"Do tell me," I urged. "Tell me what you have in your mind. Why has this cloud come up between us?"

"You see," Viola said very gently, "there are some things, if you tell a man, he is obliged to say and do certain things in return. If you take the matter in your own hands you can do better for him than he can do for himself."

"It is something for me then?" I said smiling. "I am to gain by your leaving me for a year?"

"Yes, I think so," she answered doubtfully. "But principally it is for myself. I know there is a great risk in going away, but I think a greater one if I stay."

I was silent, wondering what it could possibly be that she would not tell me. Although she said she had formed the idea before Suzee's letter came, I kept returning to that in my thoughts as the main reason that must be influencing her.

I waited, hoping if I did not press her she would perhaps begin to confide in me of her own accord. But she sat quite silent, looking intensely miserable and staring out into space before her. I felt a vague sense of fear and anxiety growing up in me.

"Dearest, do tell me what is the matter," I said, drawing her close up to me and kissing her white lips.

"Don't let us make ourselves miserable for nothing, like stupid people one reads about. Life has everything in it for us. Let us be happy in it and enjoy it."

Viola burst into a storm of tears against my neck and sobbed in a heart-breaking way for some minutes.

"Is it that you have ceased to love me, that you feel your own passion is over?" I asked gently.

"No, certainly not that."

"Is it that you think I want to, or ought to be free from you?"

"No, not that."

"Well, tell me what it is."

"I can't. I think we shall be happy again, after the year, if you let me come back to you."

I felt my anger grow up again.

"I am not going to let you leave me. I absolutely forbid it. Don't let us talk about it any more or speak of it again unless you are ready to tell me your reason."

There was a long silence, broken only by her sobs.

"Viola."

"Yes."

"Did you hear what I said?"

"Yes."

"Well, do not worry any more. You can't go, so it is settled. Nothing can hurt us while we remain together."

Viola did not say anything, but she ceased to cry and kissed me and lay still in my arms.

There was some minutes' silence, then I said:

"Let's go up to bed. Sleep will do you good. You look tired and exhausted to the last degree."

We went upstairs, and that night she seemed to fall asleep in my arms quickly and easily. I lay awake, as hour after hour passed, wondering what this strange fancy could be that was torturing her.

At last, between three and four in the morning, I fell asleep and did not wake again till the clock struck nine on the little table beside me.

The sun was streaming into the room, and I sat up wide awake. The place beside me was empty. I looked round the room. I was quite alone. Remembering our conversation of last night and Viola's strange manner, a vague apprehension came over me, and my heart beat nervously. It was very unusual for Viola to be up first. She generally lay in bed till the last moment, and always dissuaded me from getting up till I insisted on doing so. I sprang up now and went over to the toilet-table. On the back of her brushes lay a note addressed to me in her handwriting. Before I took it up I felt instinctively she had left me. For a moment I could not open it. My heart beat so violently that it seemed impossible to breathe, a thick mist came over my eyes. I took up the note and paced up and down the room for a few minutes before I could open it.

A suffocating feeling of anger against her raged through me. The sight of the bed where she had so lately lain beside me filled me with a resentful agony. She had gone from me while I slept. To me, in those first blind moments of rage, it seemed like the most cruel treachery.

After a minute I grew calm enough to tear open the note and read it.

"My very dearest one,

"Forgive me. This is the first time I have disobeyed you in anything in all the time we have been together And now βαινω. το γαρ χρην μου τε και θεων κρατει. . . .

"I must go from you, and you yourself will see in the

210

future the necessity that is ruling me now. Do not try
to find me or follow me, as I cannot return to you yet.
Do believe in me and trust me and let me return to you
at the end of this miserable year which stretches before
me now a desert of ashes and which seems as if it would
never pass over, as if it would stretch into Eternity.
But my reason tells me that it will pass, and then I
shall come back to you and all my joy in life; for there
is no joy anywhere in this world for me except with you
—if you will let me come back.

"No one will know where I am. I shall see no one
we know. Say what you wish about me to the world.

"Don't think I do not know how you will suffer at
first; but you would have suffered more if I had
stayed. While I am away from you, think of your
life as entirely your own; do not hesitate to go to Suzee,
if you wish. I feel somehow that Fate has designed
you for me, not for her, and that she will not hold
you for long, but that, whatever happens, you will
always remember

"VIOLA."

I crushed this letter in my hand in a fury of rage
when I had read it, and threw it from me. Anger
against her, red anger in which I could have killed her,
if I could in those moments have followed and found
her, swept over me.

I looked round the room mechanically. She had dressed in the clothes she had been wearing yesterday apparently, and taken one small handbag, for I missed that from where it had stood on a chest of drawers.

Her other luggage was there undisturbed. I saw her evening and other dresses hanging in the half-open wardrobe opposite me.

The only thing that had gone from the toilet-table was the little frame with my photo in it.

A sickening sense of loss, of despair came over me, mingling with the savage anger and hatred surging within me.

After a time I rose from my chair and began to dress.

I had made up my mind as to my own actions. To stay here without Viola, where the whole place spoke to me of her, was impossible. As soon as I could get everything packed I would go up to London and stay at my club. She would not come back.

No, it was no use my waiting with that hope.

Her mad scheme, whatever it was, I felt was planted deeply, her resolve fixed. It was true that three months before, after just such a cruel letter, she had come suddenly back to me, having failed in her resolution. I remembered that, and paused suddenly at the recollection. But then that was different. Then, infidelity to me had been in the question. Now I knew that wherever she was going it was not to another lover.

Whatever her foolish idea was, some benefit to me was mixed up with it in her mind.

And then, suddenly, in a tender rush of passionate reminiscence that would not be denied, the knowledge came home to me that, whatever her faults might be, however foolish and maddening her actions, no one had ever loved me as she had done, as unselfishly, with the same abandonment of self.

The hot tears came scalding up under my lids. I picked up the little crumpled sheet of paper I had so savagely crushed, smoothed it out, folded it, and put it in my breast pocket.

Then I turned to my packing. We had only taken rooms here. By paying I was free to leave at any moment.

Her things? What should I do with them? Keep them with me or send them away to her bankers?

I thought the latter, and turned to gather up her clothes and put them in her portmanteau. My brain seemed bursting with a wild agony of resentment as I took up first one thing and then another: the touch of them seemed to burn me. Then, when I was half-way through a trunk, I stopped short. Was I wise to accept the situation at all? Perhaps I could follow her and find out, after all, what this mystery meant.

We were in a small country place, but there was a fairly good service of trains to town; one I knew left in the morning at seven, she might have taken that. I could go to the station and find out.

Filled suddenly with that heart-rending longing for the sight and touch of the loved one again that is so unendurable in the first hours of separation, I thought I would do that, and I left the half-filled trunk and went downstairs to the hall.

The two maids were standing there waiting, and they stared at me as I passed and put on my hat.

"Please, sir, are you ready for breakfast? It's gone half-past ten."

"No," I said shortly. "I am going out first."

"Will Mrs. Lonsdale be coming down, sir?"

I stopped short.

"No, Mrs. Lonsdale has gone out already," I answered, and went on through the door.

I didn't care what they thought. When one is in great pain, physical or mental, nothing seems to matter except that pain.

I walked fast to the station, about a mile distant, and made enquiries as discreetly as I could.

"No," was the unanimous answer. Mrs. Lonsdale had certainly not left there by any train that morning, nor been there at all, nor hired a fly from there. They were all quite sure of that.

She was well known at the station, so it seemed improbable she could have been there unobserved.

There was another station up the line six miles distant. She might easily have walked to that to avoid notice.

I took a fly, and drove to the other station, but here Viola was not known personally, and though I described her, and was assured she had not been seen there, it was indefinite and uncertain information that settled nothing.

She might have gone from there to town by an early train unnoticed, or she might have gone down the line to another country place to elude me. I could tell nothing.

Feeling sick and dispirited, I drove back to the station and then walked on to the house.

When I went upstairs the room was in disorder just as I had left it. As I entered the bed caught my eye, the pillow her head had so lately crushed, and there beside it the delicate garment she had been wearing a few hours ago.

An immense, a devastating sense of loss came over me. A feeling of suffering so intense and so vast, it seemed to crush me beneath it physically as well as mentally.

I sank down in the arm-chair, laid my head back and closed my eyes. I ceased to think any more, I was unconscious of anything except that sense of intense suffering.

By that evening I had everything packed, all the bills paid; and I took the seven-o'clock train to town. I felt to stay there the night, to attempt to sleep in that room so full of memories of her was an impossibility. Something that would drive me mad if I attempted it.

The people of the house stared at me when I paid them, and the maids looked frightened when I addressed them, but I hardly saw them, doing what was necessary in a mechanical way, with all my senses turned inward, as it were, and blunted by that one overpowering idea of loss.

The two hours in a fast train did me good. I had a sort of subconscious feeling I was going to her by going to town which buoyed me up instinctively; but the reaction was terrible when I actually arrived and drove to some rooms I knew in Jermyn Street and realised that I was indeed alone.

I sat up all that night, feeling my brain alight and blazing with a fire of agony and pain. Sleep was out of the question. A man does not love a woman as I loved Viola and sleep the night after she has left him.

The next morning I went to her bankers, only to get just the answers I had expected.

Yes, Mrs. Lonsdale had communicated with them. She was abroad, and they had her address but were not at liberty to disclose it. They would forward all letters to her immediately.

I went straight back to my rooms and wrote to her. I poured out my whole heart in the letter, imploring her to come to me; yet every line I wrote I knew was useless, useless.

Still I could not rest nor exist till I had written it, and when it was posted I felt a certain solace.

I walked on to my club afterwards, and amongst other letters found another from Suzee.

I could not imagine how she had obtained my club address at all, unless it was in that night when she came to my cabin. She would be quite capable of searching for anything she wanted and taking away some of my letters to obtain and keep my address.

I did not open it at once. I felt a sort of anger with Suzee as being partly responsible for all I was going through. Whatever Viola might say, Suzee's letter had seemed to bring her mad resolve to a climax.

I took some lunch at the club, and a man I knew came up and spoke to me.

"Up in town again, I see," he began, to which I assented.

"How's Mrs. Lonsdale?"

"Quite well, thank you," I replied.

"Is she up with you?"

"No."

"Coming up soon, I suppose?"

"I don't know."

My friend looked at me once or twice, and then after a few vacuous remarks went away.

I knew that in a few hours it would be all over the club that I and Viola no longer hit it off together, that in fact we were living apart, and by the evening a decree *nisi* would have been pronounced for us. But I didn't care what they said. Nothing mattered. No one could hurt me more than I was hurt already. The worst had happened.

As I sat there I saw Lawton, who also belonged to the club, cross the end of the dining-room. He, too, would come up and speak to me if he caught sight of me.

I felt I did not wish to speak to the man who had always loved Viola, who had always envied me her possession, and to whom once I had nearly lost her.

I got up and left the club, went back to my rooms, and there got out my letters to read.

After all, I thought, as I took up Suzee's letter, why not go out to 'Frisco? It would make a change, something to do, something to drive away this perpetual desire of another's presence.

A second night like last stared me in the face. What was the use of continuing to feel in this wretched, angry, burning, hungry way?

I broke the seal and read Suzee's second appeal to me, more passionate, more urgent than the last. She begged me to go to her without delay, or it would be too late; a fervour of longing breathed in every line.

An ironic smile came over my face as I read. This letter to me seemed like an echo of the one I had sent to Viola that morning. Well, I would wait for her answer, and then, perhaps, if she would not return to me, I would go to 'Frisco.

In any case, I would send a few lines to Suzee with the money for her purchase. It would be best to cable it to her, and I went out again to arrange this.

Five wretched, listless days went by, followed by nearly sleepless nights, and then came Viola's answer, apparently by the postmark from some place in France.

My whole body shook as I opened it, and for many seconds I could see nothing on the paper but a mass of dancing black lines. Yet the immense comfort of being again in touch with her after these dreadful days of isolation seemed to flow over and through me like some healing balm.

At last I read these lines:

"I am terribly, unutterably grieved, my own dearest one, to hear how much you have suffered, but my return to you now would not undo that, and only give you the pain in addition that I went away to avoid for you.

"Go, dearest, go out to 'Frisco, and let the thought of me lie in your subconsciousness for a year, a little chrysalis of future happiness. Do not think of me, do not let your mind dwell on me. Fill up your life with joy and work. I have a conviction that we cannot ever really separate in this life. Therefore I do not fear (as you seemed to do) that anything will be strong enough to keep us apart if we both will to be together. Only, for a time, let me sleep in your Soul in a chamber where none other can enter, and the year will soon pass for you, though slowly, as a winter night, for me. Your

"VIOLA."

A great numbness seized me as I came to the end.

A year without her. It seemed like Eternity itself.

I sat for many hours motionless with her letter in my hand.

Then I went out and to a ticket office in Piccadilly, and got a through ticket to 'Frisco.

CHAPTER IX

IN 'FRISCO

DURING the voyage to New York and the subsequent journey across America to San Francisco I was very wretched.

The mystery of Viola's disappearance and her flight from me stood before my mind perpetually, worrying and harassing it. I felt no joyful anticipation of reaching 'Frisco and meeting Suzee, though I recognised in a dull way that some sort of distraction and companionship would be the best thing to stop this incessant pondering on the same subject. I slept little at night, and in the short intervals of rest such vivid dreams of Viola would come to me, that awakening in the morning brought a fresh anguish of despair and disappointment with it each day.

This sort of thing could not go on, I must let her "lie asleep in my subconsciousness for a year," as she put it in her letter—for to forget her was impossible— or my reason would go down under the strain.

When I arrived in San Francisco, it was one of those strange days when the sea-fog comes in to visit the town. It rolled in great thick billows down the streets from the sand dunes, obscuring everything, damping everything, filling the air with the salt scent of the open sea.

I went to one of the big hotels, and they gave me a

bedroom and sitting-room to myself: the rooms were adjoining and comfortable, but oh! what a blankness fell upon me as I sat down in one of the chairs and the bell-boy, having deposited a jug of iced water on the table, shut the door. I had been so much with Viola that it seemed strange to me now, hard to realise that I was alone. How many rooms such as these, she and I had come into, shared together, and how bright and gay her companionship had always been, how she had always laughed at the discomforts or the difficulties of our travels! Surely we had been made for each other! What strange wave of life was this that had broken us apart? I looked towards my bedroom, dull and cheerless and empty. From the open window the warm, wet, yellow fog was streaming in its soft wreaths through both rooms. The roar from the stone-paved streets, crowded with incessant traffic, came up to me muffled through the fog.

After a time I rose, closed the windows, unpacked my things, and changed my clothes. Then I went down at six to dine, as I wanted a long evening. Some champagne cheered me, and as I sat in the long, crowded dining-room, alone at my small table, my heart began to beat again warmly at the thought of the new venture before me. To-night? What would it bring forth? Should I find her? The vitalising breath of excitement began to creep through me. I finished my dinner hurriedly, swallowed my black coffee at a draught, and made my way down the room and out to the hall, putting on my hat and coat as I went. I found the guide I had asked for when I first arrived at the hotel waiting for me. He asked me mysteriously if I had put away my watch and divested myself of all jewellery, and I told him impatiently I had and showed him a small revolver I always carried. When he was somewhat reassured I took the paper that Suzee had sent me out of my pocket and showed it to him.

"That's where I want to go," I said, "and if you know every hole and cranny of the place as I was told, I suppose you know that one."

The guide grinned as he read the name.

"It's the worst place in the whole town," he remarked with a sort of admiring unction. I evidently went up in his estimation as he recognised the acumen I had shewed in my choice. I was a visitor worthy of his guidance, and he was put upon his mettle.

"The police don't dare to go there, but they'll let me in day or night."

We had reached the door now and stepped into the street. The fog had had its frolic down town, it seemed and had almost disappeared, rolling off to the sand dunes and the sea whence it had come. The night was dark and fresh with the damp saltness of the shore;

a few stars shone above. The shops were still open, and their huge plate-glass windows blazed with light. We walked rapidly through these streets towards the Chinese quarter where the noise and light ceased. The streets were quiet and empty and seemed very clean. The shops here were closed. The lights few. There was a fever of impatience in my veins. I felt as when one is drawing near to an unknown combat: a conflict the nature of which and ultimate result one does not know.

My rather shambling guide seemed amused at the pace at which I walked and giggled immoderately between remarks of his own which seemed to him to be appropriate to the occasion. I hardly heard him. At one moment I was lost in a bitter reflection of how many excursions and similar wanderings Viola had shared with me; at another, my mind seemed leaping eagerly forward, to seize this new joy in front of me.

"That's a joss-house, and that's a tea-house, and that's a silk merchant," remarked my guide at intervals, indicating different buildings as we passed. Some were frame houses with signs hanging out, painted in Chinese characters and with wonderful red door-posts; some had latticed windows with lights burning behind. But for the most part, from this outer point of view, Chinatown was clean, orderly, and dark.

FIVE NIGHTS

We stopped at last before an open doorway through which we stepped and crossed a yard, hemmed in by the crowded frame buildings round it, but open to the sky. By the light of the stars we found a ladder at the farther side and ascended this as it leant against the crooked wall of a rickety and tumbledown-looking house. The ladder went as far as the second story, where there was an open square of blackness, either window or door, through which we scrambled from the swaying rungs and then found ourselves in a passage. It was very low, apparently, for I struck my head whenever I held it upright, and so narrow that our shoulders brushed the sides. It was in fact a little tunnel, reminding one of the rounded runways a rabbit makes in thick undergrowth. It was quite dark, and my guide put himself in front and took one of my hands, pulling me along after him down steps and round corners, along different twisted, corkscrew turnings, till at last a passage a little broader than the others opened before us, where a lamp was burning; he drew back against the wall, pushing me forwards, and whispering some directions in my ear.

I passed along, as I was bid, went down two small steps, and knocked at the door I found before me. The door seemed a very stout one, securely fastened, and had a small aperture, at the height of one's face from the ground. It was only about five inches square and set with thick vertical iron bars. Behind these was an iron flap now closed.

I knocked and waited. Presently the iron flap behind the bars was cautiously opened and I saw a face peering through at me. Before I could speak the iron flap was shut to with a clank.

"That's because Nanine sees you're a stranger," whispered my guide. "They're a real bad lot here, and they're precious afraid of any 'tecs getting in. Just let me pass, sir."

I drew back, and he went up and gave the most extraordinary squawk that I ever heard. It was a pretty good password to have, for I should think no stranger could imitate it. The flap flew open again, and then some conversation ensued through the bars.

"It's all right now, sir," said the guide after a minute; "you walk right in." The door was now ajar. I went forwards and pushed it; it gave way easily. I stepped inside, and it swung to behind me. Inside the light was red—scarlet. A lamp was standing somewhere at the side of the room, behind thin, red curtains. As I entered, another door at the end of the room swung to on a retreating form. Some one had gone out. The room seemed empty. It was very small, and an enormous bed took up nearly the whole of it. There seemed no window at all anywhere: the low ceiling almost touched my head. I stopped still.

A very slight movement somewhere near me seemed to speak of another's presence.

"Suzee," I said under my breath.

At the sound of my voice there was a delighted cry, and the next moment a little form in scarlet drapery threw itself at my feet.

"Treevor, Treevor," came in Suzee's voice; and I bent over the little scarlet bundle, lifted her up, and pressed my lips on her hair. It smelt of roses, just as it had done in the tea-shop at Sitka, and carried me back there on the wings of its fragrance, as scents alone can do.

She clung to me in a wild fervour of emotion. I felt her little hands clutch me desperately. She kissed my arm and wrist passionately, seeming not to dare to lift her face to mine. This wild abandonment, this frenzy of hungered, starving love, what a sharp contrast to the cool, slow surrender of Viola, if surrender it could be called, that lending of the beautiful body, with total reserve of the spirit! Even in that moment of this wild lavishing of love from another, as the little breast leapt wildly against my own, a fierce pulse of jealous longing went through me as I thought of that unconquered something that *she* had never yielded to me.

Suzee hardly seemed to expect my caresses in return, she only seemed to wish to pour her own upon me in the wildest, most lavish excess. At last, when she grew a little calmer, I held her at arm's length from me and looked at her.

"Now, Suzee, I want you to tell me what you are doing in this awful place. How did you get here, to begin with?"

"Oh, Mister Treevor, I have had such trouble, such awful trouble, you will never believe; but when I ran—when I came to Mrs. Hackett she was very good to me, only she wanted to sell me for two hundred and fifty dollars to Chinaman. I said, 'No, I belong to rich Englishman. He send you more if you wait. He send you three hundred!' And I wrote you, you remember?"

"Yes," I answered. "Did you get the money all right that I cabled to you?"

"Oh yes, Treevor, thank you; and Nanine had it and so she was willing to keep me."

"But what have you been doing while you have been here?" I said glancing round. The whole place, with its hidden entrance, secret passages, and barred doors seemed to speak of the lowest and worst forms of vice.

"Oh, Treevor, I have been very good, so good. I would not have any visitors at all. I was so afraid you would find out and not have me if you knew, and, besides, I loved you too much." (But this was evidently an after-thought, and I noted it as such. Her true reason was given first.) "And I knew Nanine would take all my money, whatever I got. She is good to the girls here, but she takes all their money, all, they never have any. So I said to myself, 'What is the use? Besides, he will come soon and take you away.' And to Nanine I said—'Englishman will be so angry with you and with me, perhaps he will kill you or tell the police if you do not keep me for him.' And when the money came Nanine was quite pleased and said perhaps you would pay more when you came, so she did not worry me with Chinamen or any one, and I've had this room all to myself since I've been here. And I was very much afraid of you, Treevor, if I did anything at all, so I really, really have not."

I kept my eyes fixed on hers all the time she was speaking, and I felt as the words came eagerly from her lips that they were the truth. Her exquisite, un-touched beauty, her ardour of passionate welcome to me helped to illustrate it.

I smiled at her.

"Well, I am quite satisfied," I said; "I believe you have been 'good,' as you call it, because you were afraid to be otherwise. I want to hear a lot more about your husband and how you came here, but I think we had better get out of this place as soon as we can. Have you any things you want to take with you?"

"Only this," she said, pointing to an odd, little, hide-covered trunk beside her. "That has my silk clothes in it and my jewellery. If you want me to come away I can come now."

I sat silent for a moment, thinking. Where should I take her? Back to my own hotel perhaps for this one night. It might be managed. It was getting late, most of the people in the hotel would be in bed when we got there. To-morrow or the next day we could start for Mexico, where I had made up my mind to go with her.

"Very well," I said aloud; "shut up your trunk and put something round you, and we'll go now."

"You will see Nanine? You will speak to her? Let me call her," said Suzee rather anxiously. And as I assented she slipped out of the room and reappeared with a fat, coarse-looking woman who grinned amiably as she saw me. She agreed to let Suzee go with me then and there for another hundred dollars, and said her little trunk should be sent downstairs and put on a cab which the guide could get for us.

While this was being done, she chatted to me, thanked me for the money I had cabled over, and hoped I was satisfied with Suzee, her appearance, and the treatment she had received. I said I was, and asked how it was the girl had come to her at all. She seemed a little confused at that, and began to explain volubly that she had had nothing to do with it. Suzee had come there one night and begged to be taken in, and as she had known some of the girl's people who had formerly lived in Chinatown, she had done so out of pure pity and charity and love of humanity.

I listened to all this with a smile, and, as I felt I was not getting the truth, did not prolong the conversation. When the guide came back and said he was ready for us I paid the one hundred dollars and wished her good-night.

She opened the outer door of the room for us, and we went down a staircase this time which eventually led us to a door in another yard from which we gained the street. The ladder way, I take it, was used chiefly as a convenient exit in case of a raid by the police. I put Suzee into the cab and jumped in myself, the guide went on the box, and we drove back to the hotel.

It needed a certain amount of moral courage to drive up to the hotel with the scarlet-clad Suzee beside me, but I think possibly artists have a larger share of that useful quality than other men. Always having been different from others since his childhood, the artist is accustomed to the gaping wonder, the ridicule as well as the admiration, the misunderstanding, of those about him, and it ceases to affect him; while viewing as he does his companions with a certain contempt, knowing them to be less gifted than himself, he sets no store by their opinion.

So I paid and dismissed my guide, also the driver, pushed open the swinging glass doors, and entered the lounge, Suzee beside me.

We were not late enough; in another hour the hall would have been deserted. As it was, the band had ceased playing, but there were numbers of men lounging about and smoking, and groups of women still sitting in the rocking-chairs under the palms.

Through the hall we went, straight to the lift, but every eye was turned upon us and I felt rather than heard the gasp of horror that our entry caused. The elevator boy almost collapsed on the ground as I motioned Suzee to go in and sit down, which she did—on the floor.

However, no actual force was used to restrain our movements, and we reached my rooms without any hindrance.

It was decidedly an improvement to have her there; the rooms looked better, more comfortable, more as my rooms were accustomed to look.

Suzee herself was extravagantly delighted, and shewed it in every look and gesture. Gay and radiant in her brilliant scarlet silk, she moved about under the electric light like a glowing animated picture.

"What will you have to eat or drink?" I asked as I

saw her look curiously into the jug of iced water that adorned my table. "I'll order some supper."

"Anything, Treevor, anything you eat; I don't mind, and I never drink anything but tea. May I get out my own tea-things and make it?"

"Certainly," I answered, and I watched her interestedly as she went down on her knees before her little trunk and opened it, turning out beautiful coloured silks of all shades on to the floor.

While we were thus innocently engaged the hotel manager burst suddenly into the room. He looked very perturbed, and his face was a deep purple.

"Now, sir, will you tell me what you mean by behaving like this in a respectable hotel?"

He caught sight of Suzee sitting on the ground and started; the girl stared up at him with a look of astonishment in which I thought recognition blended.

"Come outside," I said mildly, "and take a turn in the corridor with me." And we both went out and shut the door.

I talked with him for fifteen minutes and explained it was unwise and unnecessary to make a great fuss and turn a good customer into the streets at this late hour. We were going in any case as soon as we could get off; in the mean time, the engagement of the next room to mine at seven dollars a day for Suzee would satisfy the proprieties. An artist must have models for his pictures and must put them up somewhere. Besides, I pointed out that he could put all my transgressions down at full length in the bill.

This seemed to soothe him very much, and our interview ended by his unlocking the door of the next room, turning on the lights, and saying what a fine one it was. I promised Suzee should occupy it, and told him we wanted supper and some champagne he could recommend. This completely softened him, and he left me promising to send the waiter for orders.

In a few minutes the same bell-boy appeared with another of the inevitable jugs of iced water, and a waiter came immediately after and took my orders. All this being temporarily arranged, I went back to Suzee. She had changed in that short time from her scarlet dress into one of the palest blue, the most exquisite soft tone of colour conceivable. It was all embroidered round the edge of the little jacket and the wide falling sleeves in mauve and silver, and she had twisted some mauve flowers and heavy silver ornaments into her shining hair. Her great dark eyes flashed and sparkled, the pure tint of her skin shewed the most faultless cream against the soft blue silk, her little mouth curved redly in gay smiles as she looked at me for admiration.

I was sad and heart-sick really in my inner self, but the senses count for much in this life and they were pleased and told me I had done well.

234

"I am quite, quite happy, Treevor," she said, as I told her she was beautiful, a vision to dazzle one. "Now see me make tea. All Chinese make it this way."

On a little side table she had rigged up a sort of spirit stand, and on this a kettle steamed merrily. Set out on the table was a queer little silver box of tea and four delicate, transparent cups or basins, for they had no handles, of the most fairy-like egg-shell china, each standing in a shell-like saucer.

"Where is your teapot?" I asked, coming up to the table and putting my hand on the blue silk-clad shoulder.

"Chinese never have teapot. That's all an English mistake. Chinese always make tea in a cup."

She took as she spoke a pinch of tea between her tiny fingers and dropped it into one of the cups, immediately filling it up with boiling water. Then she took the saucer from underneath and set it on the top, its rim exactly enclosed the edge of the cup. Raising the saucer a trifle at one side, she poured the infusion into one of the other little bowls, keeping her finger on the saucer to hold it in place. The tea leaves, kept back by the saucer, remained in the first cup. The tea, a clear, pale-amber liquid, filled the second.

"Now it is ready to drink," she said, lifting the tiny egg-shell bowl and handing it to me.

"Don't you have any milk or sugar?" I said, taking the hot basin in my hand and holding it by a little rim at the bottom, the only place one could hold it for the heat.

"No, anything else spoil it. You drink that and I make you another."

She threw away the first leaves, put a fresh pinch of tea in, filled up the bowl and strained it off into another as before, then picked up the second by the bottom rim, drained it, and repeated the process with marvellous rapidity. I watched her, sipping my own.

"Do you like it?" she asked. "It is real gold-tipped Orange Pekoe. Very good tea, indeed!"

I drank it. It had a wonderful flavour. I told her so and took another cup, to her great delight.

The waiter came in, laid our supper on the table, put the champagne in ice, and departed. I offered Suzee the wine, but she said she had all the tea she could drink. She was willing to eat, however, and we sat down to the table.

"I want you to tell me all about what happened at Sitka," I said. "How did poor old Hop Lee die?"

"Oh, it was all such a dreadful thing, Treevor," she returned, spreading out both hands, on the wrists of which heavy silver bangles set with amethysts shone and tinkled. "He went down one day to Fort Wrangle on business and when he came back one day after, he had a fearful cough, and then he got very ill and went to bed, and I sat beside him and he got worse and worse. Oh, so bad, and the doctor came and he had very much medicine, and then his chest began to bleed, and he coughed very much blood for days and days and weeks, and I nursed him all that time, Treevor, all night long. I got no sleep at all; oh, it was very, very bad."

I looked at her curiously. I could not somehow picture Suzee as the devoted nurse passing sleepless nights and never absent from the pillow of the suffering Hop Lee.

As I looked at her, I noticed the strange thickening of the features and darkening of the skin I had noted before at Sitka, and knew the blood was mounting into the face, though she could not blush, as the English girl blushes, red.

"It is really true, Treevor," she said, in an aggrieved tone.

"I am not contradicting you," I replied calmly, "go on."

"At last he died," she continued, though in rather a sulky tone, "and doctor said I might die too, I had made myself so ill, so thin with waiting on him. My bones stuck out so," she put her hands edgeways to her sides to indicate how her ribs, now remarkably well covered, had stood out from her sufferings; but remem-

237

bering the fictitious blows she had recounted to me
·when I first met her, I was not so much stirred by her
recital as I might otherwise have been.

"And what about the child?" I asked.

"The boy? Oh, Treevor, he died very soon after.
He caught cold from his father, I think."

"Did he die of cold and cough, too, then?" I asked.

"Yes, he coughed till he died. Oh, I cried so much
when he died. My baby boy, my very big baby, I
did love him so."

She blinked her glorious eyes very much as if they
were full of tears at the recollection, but I did not see
any fall, and she pursued her supper without any interruption of appetite.

I sat back in my chair, watching her and musing.
Poor old Hop Lee! I wondered what his last moments
had been like, and whether those dainty fingers had
really been employed smoothing his brow, or counting
his effects, at the last?

"And then what came after?" I asked. "How did
it come that you were to be sold, as you said?"

"We were very poor when he died; so poor, and we
owed a lot, and his brother came up from Juneau and
took over the tea-shop and everything. Then he said
he had offer from big Chinaman who would buy me,
and he said my husband owe him lot of money, he sell
me, get it back, and he sent me down to Nanine in

'Frisco to give to big Chinaman; but I told Nanine you would give more, so Nanine kept me for you."

"But how will your husband's brother get the money for you in that case?" I said.

"What a lot of questions you do ask, Treevor!" she returned sulkily. "I don't know how he will get the money. He will make Nanine give him some, I suppose. Let us forget it all, I don't want to think of that any more."

I laughed.

"Very well. If you have finished your supper, come over here and sit on my knee and we will forget it all, as you say."

She rose willingly and came over to me, a lovely, shimmering, Oriental vision, dainty and perfect.

"I must paint you, Suzee, some day just as you appear now and call you The Beauty of China, or something like that. You seem the joy of the East incarnate."

Suzee frowned and then smiled.

"I do not like such long words. I do not understand you when you talk like that; but I love you, Treevor, so, so much."

The misty light of dawn was rolling over 'Frisco when I shewed Suzee her own room, where according to the pact with the manager, she was to sleep.

She shivered as we went into it.

239

"Oh, Treevor, what a great big room," she said; "I am frightened at it. Won't you stay with me? Or let me be in yours?"

"I said you should sleep here," I answered; "so you must. Jump into bed quick and go to sleep; you will soon forget the size of the room. I am dead tired now, I must go and get some sleep myself. Goodnight, dear."

I kissed her and went back to the sitting-room. The morning light struggling with the artificial fell on the table with its scattered plates and glasses, and on her little trunk and the unpacked silken clothes.

I turned out the lights and drew up the blinds, and stood looking out. The waves of soft white fog filled the empty streets. All was quiet, white, in the dawn.

I had said I was tired, yet now sleep seemed far from my eyes, and my mind flew out over intervening space to Viola, longing to find her, wherever she was.

Where would she be? I could imagine her waking with this same dawn in her calm, innocent bed, and gazing, too, into this white light, and longing for me. Surely she would be that? The words of her letter came back to me: the time would pass "slowly as a winter night to me, your Viola."

She was right. Nothing could divide us permanently, really. Perhaps even Death would be powerless to do that.

I had a dissatisfied feeling with myself. Would it have been better, I asked myself, to have waited through this year alone, since nothing could really satisfy or delight me in her absence? What was the good, after all, of chasing the mere shadow of the joy I had with her?

But, strangely enough, I felt that Viola had no wish that I should pass this mysterious year of separation she had imposed upon us, alone.

She had confessed her inability to share my love with any other. The incident of Veronica had made that clear; but now that she chose to deny herself to me she seemed rather to wish than otherwise that I should seek adventures, experiences elsewhere. And I felt indefinitely, yet strongly, that the more I could crush into this year of life and of artistic inspiration, especially the latter, the happier she would feel when we met.

Perhaps she wished to tire me with lesser loves, certain that her own must prevail against them. Perhaps she had even left me solely for this, with this idea. Knowing herself unable to bear the pain of infidelity to her when she was present, yet, accepting it as tending to some ultimate psychological end, she had withdrawn herself from me.

I remembered she had said once to me:

"I would so much rather be a man's last love, the

crowning love of his life, the one whose image would be with him as he passed from this world, than his first; poor little toy of his youth, forgotten, unheeded, effaced by the passions of his life at the zenith."

Perhaps, . . . but, ah! what was the use of speculation when it might all be wrong?

Some reason was there, guiding that subtle mystery of her brain, and I, if I fulfilled her expressed wishes, was doing the utmost to carry out that plan of hers which I could not yet understand.

A feeling of excessive weariness invaded me, mental and physical, and as the light grew stronger, breaking into day, I went to my own room to sleep.

As soon as I woke I got up and went to look at my new possession. To my surprise the room seemed empty. I looked round. No Suzee. I went up to the bed. It had apparently not been slept in, but two of the blankets had been pulled off and disappeared.

As I stood by the bedside, wondering what had become of her, I felt a soft kiss on my ankles and, looking down, there she was, creeping out from under the bed with one of the blankets round her. Her hair was a lovely undisarranged mass; but the rosebuds in it were dead, and it was dusty. Her face looked like white silk in its youthful pallor. She smiled up delightedly at me and crawled out farther from the bed valance.

"What are you doing down there?" I asked.
"Wasn't the bed comfortable?"

"Oh yes, Treevor, underneath I was very comfortable and warm. You see, I have always been accustomed to something over my head, and in this room the ceiling is such a long way off."

She got up and stood before me, her rounded shoulders and sweetly moulded arms shewing above the blanket.

"You don't mind, do you?" she added, with a note of quick anxiety.

I laughed as I remembered the low ceilings, almost on one's head, that are the rule in Chinatown, and caught her up in my arms.

"No, I don't mind," I said; "only get into bed now, and don't shew that you have slept underneath instead of inside. I am going to order breakfast and I will call you in a minute or two."

I threw her on to the bed, into which she rolled like a kitten, kissed her, and went back to my own room.

When we had had breakfast I took Suzee with me on the car, and all the eyes of its occupants fixed upon us for the whole of the journey. This was harmless, however, and I did not mind, while Suzee sat apparently sublimely unconscious of the rude stares and ruder smiles, with the calm gravity of the Oriental who is above insults because he considers himself above criticism.

At the office where I went to buy tickets for our journey I was put to worse annoyance. I had taken tickets for two from 'Frisco to City of Mexico when the clerk, looking suddenly from me to my childish companion, said: "We can't give you a section,* sir."

"Why not?" I demanded.

"Only married couples," he remarked tersely, and turned away.

I told Suzee to go outside, and went to another part of the office, bought my section ticket from another clerk while the first was engaged, and then joined her. I began to realise that petty difficulties would line the path the whole way, and I must make some effort to minimise them.

We went to a café for lunch, and after seating ourselves at a table a little away from the staring crowd, I said: "I expect it would be better if we got you some American clothes."

"Very well, Treevor," she returned docilely, and leant her pretty, round, ivory-hued cheek on her hand as she looked across at me adoringly. Had I suggested cutting off her head, I believe she would have looked the same.

"We must try after lunch to get some," I continued. "And don't be too submissive to me in public. You see, it's not at all the fashion with us for wives to be

*Sleeping berth for two persons in the Pullman car.

that way, and it makes people think you are not mine."

Suzee laughed gaily: the idea seemed to amuse her.

After lunch we went to one of the large stores, and Suzee, in her scarlet silk attracted of course general attention. We found, however, a sensible saleswoman to whom I explained that I wanted a grey travelling costume, and she and Suzee disappeared from me entirely, into the fitting-room.

Left alone, I swung myself back on a chair and lapsed into thought.

When Suzee at last came back an exclamation broke from me. She was spoilt. Lovely as she seemed in her own picturesque clothing, in the rough grey cloth of hideous Western dress she looked simply a little guy. Reading my face at a glance, her own clouded instantly, and in another second she would have thrown herself at my feet had I not warned her by a look and a gesture not to. I sprang up and turned to the saleswoman.

"Is this the best, the prettiest costume you have?" I asked.

"Yes, sir. You see it's so difficult to fit the young lady without any corsets, and she is really so short we have only a few skirts that will do for her."

I looked at Suzee as she stood before me. The figure, so exquisite in its lines when unclothed, looked too soft and shapeless under the cloth coat. She appeared absurdly short, too, beside the American assistant, who stood at least five feet eleven. I could not bear to see my little Suzee so disfigured. However, that she looked far more ordinary could not be disputed. She would attract less attention now, and that might be an advantage. Her head was still bare and had its Oriental character, but the colour of her skin against the grey cloth.lost its creaminess that it had possessed above the blue silk jacket. It now looked merely sallow.

I paid nine guineas for the hideous dress, ordered the silk clothes to be sent to the hotel, and then we went on to the millinery. Amongst these frightful edifices my heart sank still more, but I steeled myself to the ordeal, and, choosing out the simplest grey one I could find, directed the giggling young shop-assistant to try it on Suzee.

The immense coiffure of shining black hair of the Chinese girl did not lend itself to any Western hat. Hat and hair together made her head appear out of proportion to the small, short figure.

At last, in despair, I said:

"You must alter your hair and do it in a different way. Could you take it down now and roll it up small at the back, do you think?"

Suzee gazed on me in mild surprise.

"Take my hair down, here and now! Why, it's

done up for a fortnight!" she answered simply, while the shop-girl turned away to replace a hat and hide her titters.

"Do you only do your hair once a fortnight?" I enquired, surprised in my turn.

"Yes, that's all. It's such a bother to do. It was done just before you came. I thought it would do for a month, I took such pains with it."

A month! So that beautiful, scented, shining coiffure was only brushed out once a month!

A sudden memory of Viola and her gleaming light tresses swept over me, as I had seen them at night lying on her shoulders. But had I not often waited for her till I was deadly sleepy, and when at length she came to the bedside and I had asked her what she had been doing all that time, had she not generally said—"brushing her hair"?

Perhaps, after all, a coiffure that never detained its owner at night except once a month might have its advantages.

By the time these reflections had swept over me, Suzee herself had found a little grey velvet hat that looked less dreadful than the rest. I had only to pay for it, which I did, and she walked away with me in her Western clothes. At the glove counter things went well, and she triumphed over her civilised sisters. Her tiny supple hands were easily fitted by number five,

and tired and thirsty with our efforts we left the store
and found our way to a tea-shop.

The change in dress made matters easier. She did
not attract much notice now; and unless any one looked
very closely at her, she would pass for any little ordinary,
unattractive European girl. It rather ruffled my vanity
to think she should look like this, but I consoled myself with thinking of the evening, when the hideous
disguise could be laid aside and she would appear
again in her amber beauty and I could pose her in a
hundred ways.

We had several cups of tea apiece. Very good I
found it, though Suzee somewhat disdainfully remarked it was not like China tea; and then returned to
the hotel.

As I passed through the swing doors with my re-
clothed and much altered companion, the proprietor
came hastily forwards with protestation written on his
face. He evidently thought I had erred again and
this was another investment. He was about to im-
part vigorously his opinion of me when a hasty glance
at Suzee's face and my bland look of enquiry stopped
him. Instead of addressing us, he wheeled round dis-
comfited and disappeared into his bureau.

"Why does that man always look so crossly at you?"
enquired Suzee, as we were walking down the passage
to our rooms.

"He does not approve of my wickedness in having you here," I answered laughing. "He thinks a man must never be with any woman but his wife."

"And has he a wife?"

"Yes, that great creature you saw sitting in the glass desk downstairs."

Suzee threw up her chin and pursed up her soft blue-red lips.

"I know that man by sight quite well. He was always down with the girls in Chinatown. He was one of Nanine's best customers."

I laughed as I put the key in, and opened our door.

"That accounts then, quite, for his terrific propriety in his hotel," I answered. "It's always the way. You can tell the really vicious person by his affected horror of vice."

We dined upstairs, and directly after dinner I got her to pose for me that I might catch the first idea for my picture "The Joy of the East."

She still shewed an apparently unconquerable objection to any undraped study, so I did not press it, but told her to dress as she had been dressed the previous night, in blue and mauve with silver ornaments, and I would take her in that.

While she was arraying herself I sat back in my chair, thinking.

How strange it was that a girl like Viola, who I

believed would have been burnt alive rather than let an untruth pass her lips, who could not possibly have done a dishonourable action, had posed for me so simply and fearlessly, viewing the whole matter from that artistic standpoint which is so lofty because so really pure; and this girl, whose soul, as I knew, was full of trickery and treachery, and whose lips were worn with lies, clothed herself about with this ridiculous prudery and imagined it was modesty!

She came back presently, wonderfully lovely in the bizarre Oriental costume, and I wanted her to stand on tiptoe, leaning towards me and laughing.

But she was not a good model; she soon grew tired and failed to keep the same pose or expression. She fidgeted so, that at last I laid the paper aside.

"Your expression won't go with that title," I said. "What is the matter? Can't you stand still and look happy for fifteen minutes?"

"It's so tiring to stand quite still," she said crossly, and my heart reproached me as I thought of Viola and the hours she had stood for me without a word of complaint in the London studio!

"Well, I'll try another picture. I shall call it 'The Spoiled Favourite of the Harem.' Throw yourself into that chair and look as cross as you like."

Suzee sat down opposite me. I put her head back against the chair; her right arm hung over the side, in her left hand she held a cigarette, one foot was bent under her, the other swung listlessly to the ground.

Her expression, restless and dissatisfied, her attitude, weary and enervated, gave the idea of the title admirably, and I made a good sketch.

She was sitting down now so she could keep still without much difficulty, and her air of *ennui* suited this theme well enough.

As soon as I had finished the sketch and told her she might get up she was delighted. She did not seem to take much interest in the picture, however, but rather regard it grudgingly as it took up my attention. She was only happy again when I took her on my knees and caressed her, telling her she was the loveliest Eastern I had ever seen.

The following day we started on our journey southward.

CHAPTER X

IN THE SHADOW OF THE VOLCANO

THE journey down to the City of Mexico, in itself, was a delight to me, and I felt how infinitely more I could have enjoyed it had Viola been with me.

My present companion did not seem able to appreciate any but physical beauty. If a good-looking man came on board the train she glanced over him, demurely enough, but with the eye of a connoisseur. The glorious beauty, however, of the painted skies and magnificent stretches of open country we were passing through affected her not at all.

For four days, on either side of the train, America unrolled before us her vast tracts of entrancing beauty, from which I could hardly tear my gaze, and this little almond-eyed doll sat in a lump on the seat opposite me yawning and fidgeting, or else reading some childish book; or spent the time at the other end of the car playing with some American children on board the train.

I did not intend to have my journey spoilt by her, so I gave my own attention to the scene and told her to go and play, if she wished, or buy oranges and pictures from the train-venders, do anything she liked, in fact, as long as she did not disturb me and prevent my taking a pleasure in the beauty she could not see.

Suzee, annoyed at my admiration of something she

could not appreciate, was mostly sulky and pettish through the day, regaining her good temper at night when we retired into our section.

As a toy to caress, to fondle, she was enchanting. Nature had apparently made her for that and for nothing else. Her extreme youth, her beauty, her joy in love, made her irresistible at such moments. And as I was young, at the height of youth's powers and desires, our relations in that way held a great deal of pleasure for us both.

But that was the limit. Beyond this there was nothing.

That exquisite mental companionship, that sharing of every thought and idea, that constant conversation on all sorts of subjects that interested us both, all this which I had had with Viola, and which filled so perfectly those intervals when the tired senses ask for, and can give, no more pleasure, was completely absent here.

That delight in beauty which is to an artist as much a part of his life as another man's delight in food or wine Viola had shared with me in an intense degree.

And sharing any of the delights of life with one we love enhances them enormously. One can easily imagine a gourmand being dissatisfied with his wife if she resolutely refused to share any of his meals!

Now, as I gazed through the windows of the

slow-moving train and saw the long blue lines of the level-topped hills, the deep purple edges of the vast table-lands rising against the amber or the blood-red evening skies, I longed for Viola with that inward longing of the soul which nothing but the presence of its own companion can satisfy.

One evening, as I gazed out, the whole prairie was bathed in rose-coloured light that appeared to ripple over it in pink waves. The tall grass, tall as that of an English hay-field, seemed touched with fire; far on every side stretched the open plain, absolutely level, bounded at last in the far distance by that deep purple wall of mountains, flat-topped, level-lined also, against the sky, the great mesas or table-lands of Mexico.

And in this vast expanse of waving grasses and low flowering shrubs, in the pink glow of the evening, stood out two graceful forms, a pair of coyotes, distinct against the sunset behind them. Only these two were visible in all that great lonely plain, and they stood together watching the train go by, their sinuous bodies and low sweeping tails touched and tipped with fire in the ruby light.

How delighted Viola would have been with that scene, I thought regretfully, as the train carried us through it.

When we arrived at the City of Mexico, we drove to the Hotel Iturbide and took a room high up on the third floor, to be well lifted out of the suffocating atmosphere of the streets.

Suzee was a little overawed by the height of the long, narrow room that we had assigned to us in this, at one time, palace, but when she saw that the bed was comfortable and there was a large mirror before which she could array and re-array herself, she was satisfied.

I saw the room would be a very difficult one to paint in, for it was dark in spite of the tall window which opened on to an iron balcony running across the front of the hotel.

The window was draped with thick red curtains and had a deep, handsome cornice hanging over it.

Suzee went on to the balcony immediately and was delighted with the incessant stream of gaily dressed people passing underneath. This was the main street of the city. Not very wide, flanked with lofty, old, picturesquely built houses on each side, of which the lower part was often shop or restaurant, it presented somewhat the same heavy, gloomy appearance as the streets in Italian towns. The air was thick, dust-laden, and evil-smelling, for the City of Mexico, though at an elevation of 8,000 feet, has none of the crisp, healthful clearness, usually to he found at that altitude. Built over the bed of an enormous dried-up lake, in the centre of an elevated table-land, it is, even at the present day, badly drained and unhealthy.

We had some tea brought up to us and took it at a little table drawn close to the window,—Suzee chattering away to me of the delights of this new big city —as big as 'Frisco, she thought. And what gay hats the women wore! She saw them passing underneath. Would I not take her out to the shops and buy a great big white muslin hat like theirs, covered with pink roses?

I promised I would, watching her with a smile.

She was certainly very lovely just now. She seemed to have bloomed into fairer beauty than she had possessed at Sitka.

Doubtless her gratified passion and happy relations with me helped to this result, for a woman's beauty depends almost wholly on her inner life, the life of her emotions and passions.

After tea we went downstairs, hired a carriage, and drove to the Paseo—or laid-out drive—which is the thing to do in Mexico at that hour; and to follow the custom of the country you are in is the first golden rule of the traveller who would enjoy himself.

It was about six o'clock, and darkness was closing in on the thick, dust-filled air as we drove with the stream of other vehicles of all descriptions, from the poorest hired carriage to the most splendidly appointed barouche, into the Paseo, a wide, sweeping drive, lined each side with trees and lighted with rows of electric

arc-light lamps, some of which glowed pinkly or sput-
tered out blue rays in the dusk.

It has never seemed to me a very cheerful matter,
this drive between the lights in the formal Paseo,
this great string of carriages drawn mostly by poor
unhappy horses and filled ¦with dressed-up women
who stare rudely at each other as they pass and
re-pass, solemn and silent ghosts in a world of grey
shadow!

But the fashion amongst the Mexican women of
painting and powdering to an inordinate degree perhaps accounts for their love of this hour between the
lights, when they imagine the falseness of their com-
plexion cannot be detected.

After about an hour's drive we came back, the great
arc-lights now sending their uncertain, shifting glare
across the road and serving to show the heavy dust
through which we moved. Seen sideways, the ray of
light looked solid, so thick was the atmosphere.

When we came back we dined, and then sat outside
our window on the iron balcony, looking down at the
gay scene below.

The street was fully lighted now by powerful lamps
of electricity, some belonging to the roadway, others
hung out over restaurants and shops. The latter were
all open, having been closed through the middle of the
day. The cafés and restaurants were in full swing,

half the populace seemed in the street, either walking or driving.

"We will go to a theatre as soon as they open," I said. "I don't think any of them begin till half-past nine or ten."

Suzee clapped her hands.

"That will be nice, Treevor," she said.

"I did like the theatre in Chinatown. I went with Nanine sometimes."

So at half-past nine we drove to a theatre. The performance began at ten o'clock and continued till one in the morning, with a break in the middle for supper.

It was a light musical farce, well acted and sung, and I enjoyed it.

Suzee looked on profoundly silent, and seemed to be quite wide-awake all through it. Just before one o'clock she leant to me and whispered:

"When does the killing begin?"

"Killing?" I returned. "I don't think there'll be any, what do you mean?"

"Oh," she said, "in Chinese theatres there is always very much killing; every one's head comes off at the end."

I laughed.

"You little monster," I whispered; "is that what you came to see?" Suzee nodded.

"All Chinese plays like that," she answered.

We waited till the curtain fell, but there was no killing and all the heads were left on at the end. Suzee looked quite disappointed, and explained to me as we were driving away that that was no play at all.

The next morning we were up very late, and after breakfast in our room there was only time to drive out to the shops and buy for Suzee one of the hats she coveted before luncheon.

All Orientals have a wonderful, artistic instinct for fabrics and colours, and always, when left alone, clothe themselves with exquisite taste. But this instinct seems to desert them when brought amongst European manufactures and into the sphere of European tints. Suzee now chose an enormous white hat wreathed round with poppies and cornflowers that I certainly should not have chosen for her. However, it pleased and satisfied her, and she was in great good-humour in consequence.

I found some letters for me at the hotel, forwarded from the club. My heart sank as I saw there was none from Viola. I thought she might have written again. . . .

There was one from a friend of mine who was attached to the embassy here, and he asked me to go and dine with him that evening, or name some other, if I were engaged that day.

I looked up at Suzee.

"I have an invitation here to go out to dinner," I said to her; "do you think you can amuse yourself without me this evening?"

Suzee looked sulky.

"You are going out all the evening without me? Can't I come too?"

"I am afraid not," I answered.

"Why? Is it a woman you are going to?"

"No, it is not," I answered a little sharply.

How different this sulky questioning was from Viola's bright way of assenting to any possible suggestion of mine for my own amusement or benefit!

How different from this her quick:

"Oh yes, do go, Trevor, do not think about me, I shall be quite happy looking forward to your coming back!"

Suzee pushed out her lips.

"How long will you be?" she asked.

"I shall go just before seven and return about ten," I answered. "You must get accustomed to amusing yourself. I can't always be with you."

"I can amuse myself," returned Suzee sulkily. "All the same, I believe it's a woman you are going to."

The blood rushed over my face with anger and annoyance, but I restrained myself and made no answer. She was so much of a child, it seemed absurd to enter into argument or to get angry with her.

I went back to reading my other letters and occupied myself with answering them till luncheon.

That evening about seven I was dressing for dinner, Suzee standing by me or playing with my things and somewhat impeding me, as usual. She seemed to have recovered from her ill-temper and was all smiles and gay prattle.

Before I took up my hat and coat to leave I bent over her and kissed her.

"You understand, I don't want you to leave this room till I come back. They will bring up your dinner here, and you can sit on the balcony and smoke, and you have lots of picture-books to amuse you. I shall be back at ten."

She kissed me and smiled and promised not to leave the room, and I went out.

I really enjoyed the evening with my friend. It was a relief to talk again with one who possessed a full-grown mind after being so long with a childish companion, and the time passed pleasantly enough. A quarter to ten seemed to come directly after dinner and my companion was astonished at my wanting to leave so early.

I explained the situation in a few words and, of course, caused infinite amusement to my practical friend.

"The idea of you living with a Chinese infant like

that!" he exclaimed. "I shall hear of your being fascinated with a Hottentot next, I suppose."

"Maybe," I answered, putting on my hat. "Anyway, I must go now; thanks all the same for wishing me to stay."

I left him and walked rapidly back in the direction of the Iturbide. Some of the shops were still open, and as I passed down the main street the brilliant display in a jeweller's window, under the electric light, attracted my attention.

I paused and looked in. I thought I would buy and take back some little thing to Suzee. It had been a dull evening for her. I went in and chose a necklet of Mexican opals. These, though not so lovely as the sister stone we generally buy in England, have a rich red colour and fire all their own.

I had not enough money with me to pay for it, but with that delightful confidence in an Englishman—often unfortunately misplaced—one finds in some distant countries, the shopman insisted on my taking it, and said he would send to the hotel in the morning for the money.

I slipped the case in my pocket and went on to the Iturbide.

After all, I thought, as I neared home, with all her faults she was a very attractive and dear little companion to be going back to.

Full of pleasure at the thought of bestowing the gift and the joy it would give her, I ran up the stone stairs without waiting for the lift and pushed open the door of our room.

I entered softly, thinking she might be curled up asleep, but as I crossed the threshold I heard the sound of laughter. The next moment I saw there were two figures standing at the end of the long room in front of the window.

Suzee had her back to me and a man was standing beside her. Just as I came in I saw her raise her face, and the man put his arm round her and kiss her. Two or three steps carried me across the room and I struck them apart with a blow on the side of the man's head that sent him reeling into a corner.

It was the young Mexican waiter that had hitherto brought us all our meals.

The table was still covered with the dinner things, a bottle of wine stood on it and two half-filled glasses. My impression, gathered in that first furious glance, was that he had brought up her dinner and she had invited him to stay and share at least the wine and cigarettes. Some of these lay on the table, and the room was full of smoke.

Suzee gave a scream of terror and then crouched down on a chair, looking at me.

The waiter picked himself up, and, catching hold

of his iron stove-fitted basket in which he had brought up the dinner, slunk out of the room.

I was left alone with Suzee, and I looked at her, with an immense sense of disgust and repulsion swelling up in me.

"So you can't even be trusted an hour or two, it seems," I said contemptuously, throwing myself into a chair opposite her.

Suzee began to sob. Tears were her invariable refuge under all circumstances.

"Treevor, you were so long. I was all alone, and I was sure you were with another woman."

"If you would learn to believe what I say and not fancy every one tells lies, as I suppose you do," I answered hotly, "it would be a great deal better for you. I went to dine with a bachelor friend this evening, as I told you, and what made me later than I otherwise should have been was that I stopped to buy a present for you on my way back."

Suzee's tears dried instantly.

"A present! Oh, what is it, Treevor?" she said eagerly. "Do show it me. Where is it?"

I drew the case out of my pocket and opened it. The electric light flashed on the opals, and they blazed with orange and tawny fires on the white velvet.

Suzee gave a little cry of wonder and delight, and then sat staring at them breathlessly.

"I don't feel at all inclined to give them to you now," I remarked coldly.

"Oh, yes, Treevor, *do* let me have them. It was all the man's fault. I did not want him. I could not help it."

"I heard you laughing as I came in," I returned, more than ever disgusted by her lies and her throwing all the blame on her companion. "It's no use lying to me, Suzee, you found that out at Sitka. What I want to make clear to you is this: if I find you doing this sort of thing again I shall send you away from me altogether, because I won't have it."

Suzee looked terror-stricken.

"Send me away! But what could I do? Where could I go?"

"Where you pleased! You would not live any more with me."

"Well, Treevor, I will not do it any more," she answered, her eyes fixed on the jewels. "Do let me have the necklace. May I put it on?"

And she stretched out her hand to grasp it from the table where I had laid it. Her avarice, her lack of any real deep feeling about the matter, filled me with irrepressible anger.

I sprang to my feet and snatched the necklet up, case and all, and flung it through the window.

"No, you shall certainly not have it," I exclaimed.

Suzee gave a shriek of pain and dismay as she saw the beloved jewels flash through the air and disappear in the darkness, and rushed to the window as if she would jump after them.

Fearing she might call to the passers-by below and create a disturbance, I took her by the shoulder and pulled her back into the room.

Then I shut the window and bolted it above her head.

I walked over to the door of the room.

"You had better go to bed," I said; "do not wait for me, I shall sleep elsewhere."

Then I went out and locked the door behind me, putting the key in my pocket.

I went down the passage slowly. My heart was beating fast and I felt angry, but the anger was not that deep fierce agony of emotion I had felt at times when Viola angered or grieved me.

It was more a superficial sensation of disgust and repulsion that filled me, and, after a few minutes, I grew calm and recovered my self-possession.

"What could I expect from a girl like this?" I asked myself. "What could I expect but lies and deceit and trickery and infidelity? She had shewn me all these at Sitka when I first met her."

I had been willing enough to profit by them, but even then they had disgusted me. Now I was in the

266

position of Hop Lee, and as she had treated him so would she treat me. It was true she professed to love me, and did so in her way. But it was the way of the woman who is bought and sold.

And why should I feel specially repelled because I had found her with a servant? Had she not come from a tea-shop in Sitka, where she herself was serving?

The Mexican boy was handsome enough. Doubtless he presented a temptation to her.

It was all my own fault, everything that had happened or would happen, for choosing such an unsuitable companion. The light loves of an hour with painted butterflies such as Suzee are well enough, but for life together one must seek and find one's equal, one who sees with the same eyes, who has the same standard as one's own of the fitness of things, in whose veins runs blood of the same quality as one's own.

Why had Viola left me? The thought came with a pang of anguish as my heart called out for her.

The corridor was a lofty one of stone. It was quite empty now and unlighted. I walked on slowly in the dark till I came to a large window on my right hand. This window overlooked a wide expanse of lead roofs belonging to the lower stories of the hotel, and these commanded a magnificent view of the whole city.

I stepped out over the low sill and stood on the

leads. The night was soft and cool. The sky, full
of the light of a rising moon, shewed beautifully, against
its luminous violet, the outlines of dome and minaret
and spire, and far out beyond the crowded city's con-
fines, the two incomparable mountains, Popocatepetl
and Ixtaccihuatl, the huge volcanoes, shrouded in eternal snow, rising a sheer ten thousand feet from the
level plain, standing like sentinels guarding the city.

It was a magnificent panorama that surrounded
me, a view to remember for all time. Dome upon
dome, rising one behind the other, of all sizes and
shapes, their beautiful tiles gleaming here and there
as the light from the rising moon touched them, delicate spires, pointing upwards, tipped with silver light,
low roof of the commoner's dwelling and pillared façade of old and stately palace intervening, and, far
away, those cold white, solitary peaks overtopping all
else, rising into the region of the stars, made up a
grand, impressive scene.

As I looked all sense of petty annoyance dropped
from me. I walked forwards with a grateful sense of
relief and took my seat on a projecting ledge of one
of the roofs and let my eyes wander over the maze of
dim outlines and shapes below me.

How strange it was to think of the past history of
the city!

Far back in the dim ages, a clear and glorious lake

had lain here where now the city reared itself so majestically. In the centre of this vast table-land, eight thousand feet above the sea, the blue waters rested tranquilly, reflecting in their surface the fires and the flames of those now silent, burnt-out volcanoes.

The lake was inhabited by the lake-dwellers, quaint little people living in their curious structures built on poles sunk in the water. There they fished and made their nets and traded with each other, passing backwards and forwards in their tiny dug-outs—whole crafts made from a single hollowed-out log—on the gleaming waters, secure from the raids of wild beasts or savages that the black, impenetrable forests on the shore might harbour.

Then came the Toltecs and the Aztecs with their refinement, their civilisation, and the lake dried gradually through the years, and causeways were built across the swamp, and one by one dwellings appeared on the hardest, driest places, and step by step there grew to be a city. Then came the Spaniards in later days, with the flaming pomp of religion and the loathsome spirit of cruelty. They killed the people by thousands with torture, and set up their churches to peace and good-will. They overthrew the temples with murder and slaughter, and reared altars to the Most High on the blood-soaked earth.

And this city, as we see it to-day, with its countless

beautiful churches, its exquisite tiled domes flashing in the sun, is the work of the Spaniards. And each church stands there to commemorate their awful crimes.

I sat on, as the hours passed, and watched the moon rise till it poured its flood of silver light all over the city, sat thinking on the horror of man and wondering what strange law has fashioned him to be the devil he is.

Towards sunrise, the wind blew cold off the marshes round the city, and I went in and down to the lower floor of the hotel.

Its world was fast asleep. In the hall I saw two Mexican porters in their thin white clothes, curled up on the door mat, without covering or pillow, fast asleep.

I made my way to the little-used reception-room, found my way across it to a wide old couch, threw myself upon it, and closed my eyes. The couch smelt musty and the room seemed cold, but I was accustomed to sleep anyhow and anywhere, and in a few moments, with my thoughts on Viola, I drifted into oblivion.

At breakfast time the next day I went to the administrador and told him to send up ours by another waiter, and never to allow the former one to come into our room again. Then I went upstairs to Suzee. As I unlocked the door and entered I saw she was up and dressed. She came to me, looking white and frightened.

"Oh, Treevor, do forgive me, I never will again. Only say you forgive me. I was so frightened all last night, I thought you had locked me up here to starve."

Again the absence of deep feeling, of any ethical consideration prompting her contrition, jarred upon me. She would be good because she did not want to starve or be otherwise punished. That was her view of it, and that alone.

I bent over her, took her hand, and kissed her.

"We needn't think of it any more," I said gently. "Only you must remember if such a thing occurs again, we cease to live together, that's all."

Suzee reiterated her promises with effusion, and presently an old, grey-haired waiter appeared with our breakfast.

I could not repress a smile as I saw the administrador had determined to be on the safe side this time.

Suzee was extremely amiable and docile all that day.

Most women who do not shew gratitude for kindness and consideration, when the man retaliates or shews any harshness, begin to improve wonderfully; while a delicate nature like Viola's, that responds to love and gives devotion in return, would meet that same harshness with passionate resentment. Suzee sincerely mourned her lost jewels and gazed wistfully and furtively down into the street where they had gone in the darkness.

I paid the bill for them that day, but I never knew what became of them, nor whose neck they now adorn!

The following day was Sunday, the day appointed by the Prince of Peace, and dedicated here by his followers, the Christians, to the torture and slaughter of their helpless companions in this world—the animals. Sunday, throughout Mexico, is the day most usually fixed for a bull-fight, and to-day there was going to be one, and Suzee had begged me to take her to see it.

I had hesitated, but finally given in, and taken seats for it.

I felt a strong disinclination to witnessing what I knew would be merely another example of the loathsome barbarity of the human race, but it was my rule in life to see and study its different aspects, to add to my knowledge of it whenever possible, and so I consented with a sense of repulsion within me. Suzee was in the wildest delight. She had talked to the waiter, it seemed, and had heard from him wonderful stories of the big crowds of gaily dressed people in the large ring, of the music, of the gaily dressed toreadors, of the clapping of hands and the shouting.

"And you feel no sympathy with the bull that is going to be killed or the unfortunate horses?" I asked, looking across at her as we sat at luncheon.

Suzee looked grave.

"I didn't think of that," she said.

The great fault of the less guilty half of humanity —it does not think! and the other half thinks evil.

"Well, think now," I said sharply. "Would you like to have your inside torn out for a gaping crowd to laugh at, to be tortured to death for their Sunday diversion? For that is what you are going to see inflicted on the animals this afternoon."

Suzee regarded me with a frightened air.

Presently she said, glibly:

"Of course not, Treevor, and I am very, very sorry for the poor animals if they are going to be hurt."

"Of course they are," I said shortly; "that is what the whole city is going to turn out to see."

I felt she had no real appreciation of the subject, and that any sympathetic utterance would be made to please me. How I hate being with a companion who automatically says what will please me! A servile compliance that one knows is false is more irritating to a person of intellect than contradiction.

How different Viola had always been! In physical relations she had accepted me as her owner, master, conqueror. She had never sought to deny or evade or resent the physical domination Nature has given the male over the female. But her mind had been always her own. And what a glorious strength and independence it possessed! Not even to me would she ever have said what she did not believe.

Like the old martyrs, she would have given herself to the rack or the flames rather than let her lips frame words her brain did not approve.

Her mind and her opinions were her own, not to be bought from her at any price whatever, and, as such, they were worth something.

The assent or dissent of the fool who agrees or disagrees from fear or love is worth nothing when you've got it.

We finished our luncheon and then, in a hired carriage, drove to the Plaza de Toros.

I, with a feeling of cold depression, Suzee, gaily dressed and in the highest spirits.

All the city was streaming out in splendid carriage or miserable shay. Rich and cultured, poor and illiterate, human beings are all alike in their love of butchery and blood. We reached the great ragged stretch of open ground, hideous and bare enough, and the structure of the bull-ring reared itself before us, a sinister curve against the laughing blue of the sky.

It seemed to hum like a great hive already; there was a crowd of the poorer class about it, and men came continually in and out of the little doors in its base.

We dismissed our carriage at the outer edge of the ragged ground, the driver insisting he could drive no farther. And the moment we had alighted he turned his horses' heads and started them at a furious gallop back to the city in the hope of catching another fare.

We walked forwards towards the principal of the wickets through which already the people were passing to their seats. In approaching the bull-ring we had to pass by a circle of little buildings, low dens with small barred windows and closed doors. Blood was trickling from under some of these over the brown and dusty earth, and the low, heavy breathing and groans of a horse in agony came from one or another at intervals.

I looked through the grated slit of one, as I passed, and saw two men, or, rather, fiends in the shape of men, crouched on the floor of the dark and noisome den. Between them lay outstretched the body of a horse, old and thin, worn to the last gasp in the cruel service of the streets. On its flank was a long open wound. One of the men, bending over it, had a red-hot iron glowing in his hand. What they were going to do I could not tell, and I did not wait to see.

The horse was one, doubtless, which unhappily had survived last Sunday's bull-fight, and was being horribly patched up, terribly stimulated by agony to expend its last spark of vitality in this.

In these loathsome little dens this fiendish work goes on, the poor mangled brutes are brought out from the ring, their gaping wounds are plugged with straw, or anything that is at hand, and then they are thrust back on to the horns of the bull.

More than ever filled with loathing of my kind, I passed on in silence towards the ring.

It was no use speaking to Suzee. She could not understand what I felt. I thought of Viola. If she had been here, what would she have suffered? Of all women I had met, I had never known one who had the same exquisite compassion, the same marvellous sympathy for all living things as she had.

We shewed our tickets, passed through the wicket, and were inside the vast circle.

The impression on the eye as one enters is pleasing, or would be if one's brain were not there to tell one of the scenes of infamy that take place in that grand arena.

Wide circles, great sweeping lines have always a certain fascination, and the form that charms one in the coliseum is here also in these modern imitations.

The huge arena, empty now and clean, sprinkled with fine white sand, and with circle after circle, tier after tier of countless seats rising up all round, cutting at last the blue sky overhead, is in itself impressive.

We passed to our seats, which were a little low down, not much raised above the level of the boarding running round the arena.

They were on the coveted shady side of the ring, where the sun would not be in our eyes. On the left of us was the President's box; opposite, the seats of the common people, let cheap, because the sun's rays would fall on them through all the afternoon.

These were already full. Occupied by *women*, largely *women*. Dressed in their gayest, with handkerchiefs in their hands ready to wave, with brightly painted fans, they sat there laughing, talking, eating sweets, making the ring in that quarter a flare of colour.

Women! Ah, what a pity it is that there should be such women as these, stony-hearted, stony-eyed, deaf to the dictates of mercy, of pity. Women who can congregate with delight to see a fellow-creature die!

For what are the animals but our fellow-creatures? With the same life, the same heart-beats as our own! With whom, if we acted rightly, we should share this world in kindly fellowship and love.

The other seats in the shade were filling quickly; soon the whole mass of dizzy circles, one above the other, flamed with brilliant colour under the Mexican sun.

Suddenly, with a great crash, the music burst out, and a triumphal march rolled over the arena as the President and his party arrived and took their places in their box. The people cheered and the handkerchiefs were waved, for the President is popular.

Suzee sat in the greatest glee beside me. The vast

concourse of people, the lavish colour, the loud, gay, strident music, the sea of faces and clapping hands and waving kerchiefs pleased her childish little soul.

After a few moments the music changed, and to a slow, almost solemn march, the toreadors filed slowly in to the arena and bowed before the President's box.

A burst of applause greeted their appearance, and Suzee watched entranced these men parading in the ring, in their various red, blue, and green velvet costumes fitting tightly their fine figures, with their gorgeous cloaks of red velvet thrown over one arm and the flat round hats of the toreadors sitting lightly above their bold handsome faces.

They disappeared, there was a pause in the music, the great arena stood empty, the vast audience were silent, a few moments of waiting expectancy, then one of the low doors opposite us in the inner circle flew open, shewing a long black tunnel leading into darkness. From this came confused roarings and bellowings, and then with his head flung high and his great eyes starting with pain and rage from the goadings he had received, a glorious black Andalusian bull charged into the arena. The people, delighted at his size and strength and apparent ferocity, cheered and applauded loudly while, still further excited by the sudden glare of light and the deafening noise, the creature galloped round the sandy ring.

Jet-black, sleek-coated, and with a long pair of slender, tapering horns, sharply pointed, crowning his great head, he was a magnificent animal, far finer in make and shape than any of these brutes round him who had come to see him die. As he galloped round the ring, I saw that he was looking wildly, eagerly, for somewhere to escape. The animals have no innate savagery, as man has. They do not love inflicting pain, torture, and death upon others. That vile instinct has been given to man alone. They kill for food. They fight for their mates. But no animal fights or kills for the love of blood as we do.

And now this great monarch of the hills and plains, in all the pride and glory of his strength, had no wish to attack or kill; he bounded round and across the sandy space hoping to find some outlet, longing to be again upon his wild Andalusian hills he was never to see again.

Another burst of music, a great fanfare of trumpets, and then slowly in triumphal procession the picadors, mounted bull-fighters with lances, entered the ring.

Theoretically, when these men enter, the savage beast they are supposed to be encountering immediately makes a terrible charge upon them; but, as a matter of fact, the bull never wishes to fight or attack any one, and does not, until his brutal captors absolutely force him into doing so. That is why a bull-fight, as well as being hideously degrading and cruel, is also dull and tedious.

If one were watching the grand natural passion of an animal fighting for his life on the prairie, against another, with an equal fortune of war for both, there would be excitement in it. But in this case one sees an unwilling animal tortured into a fight, which it neither seeks nor understands, and which it has from the start no chance of winning.

In this case, as in all I have seen, the beautiful Andalusian, having made his gallop round the ring and finding no chance of escape, had subsided into a quiet trot and when the picadors entered he stood still, demurely regarding them from the opposite side of the arena.

The sunlight fell full upon him, on his glossy sides and grand head, from which the noble, lustrous brown eyes looked out with benign and gentle dignity on the great multitude, the sandy space, and the picadors who were stealing slowly up to him.

It is a difficult matter for the picador to approach the bull, for the horses shrink from the awful fate awaiting them, and only by plunging great spurs into their sides can their riders get them to advance.

Anything more unutterably cowardly and despicably mean than the picador can hardly be imagined. Riding a poor, aged horse, generally one that has been wounded in a previous combat, and that is absolutely naked of all protection from the bull's horns, he is himself cased from head to foot in metal and leather, so that by no possibility can he be scratched.

He comes into the ring with the deliberate intention of riding his tottering, naked horse on to the horns of the bull, and the greater number of these helpless creatures he can get mangled and disembowelled under him, the greater and finer picador he is and the more the people love him. Such is humanity!

On this afternoon the bull eyed the horses' approach with no ill-will, he seemed to be reflecting—"Perhaps these are friends of mine and will show me the way out." But when at last the picador, having spurred his flinching horse close up to the bull's side, jabbed at his glossy neck with his lance and the pain convinced the great monarch they were hostile, he threw up his head with a snort and in a lithe, agile bound he passed by them and trotted quietly away.

This enraged the people, and screams of "Coward! Coward!" went up from all parts of the ring.

How they can twist into any semblance of cowardice the benignity of an animal that scorns to take any notice of what it sees is a feeble and puny opponent is amazing, a fit illustration of the weakness of the human intellect.

As the bull continued his gentle trot, unmoved, the

audience grew furious, and then began that tedious
and utterly sickening chase of the unwilling bull by
the faltering and unwilling horses.

The bull, conscious of his great strength and absolutely fearless, had all that chivalry which seems inherent
in animals and which is quite lacking in man in his
attitude to them.

As the unfortunate horses were ridden up to and
across the face of the bull, he did his best to avoid
them. Over and over again the picadors stabbed
him with their lances and thrust their naked horses at
his head, but his whole attitude and manner said plainly:
"Why should I toss these poor old, trembling horses?
I have no quarrel with them. I could kill them in a
minute, but I don't want to."

The screaming fiends above him yelled and cursed
and tore pieces of wood from the seats to throw at him.
Insults and invectives were showered on the picadors,
until at last one of them, stung by the filthy abuse of the
mob, drove his spurs so deep into his horse that the
animal reared a little; the picador then, with spur and
knee, almost lifted him on to the long pointed horns of
the bull, who, forced back against the hoarding, had
lowered his head in anger as the blood streamed from
the lance wounds in his neck.

Then there was the horrid, low sound of grating
horn against the ribs of the horse, the ripping of the

hide; the animal was lifted into the air a moment, then fell. There was a gush of blood on the sand, blood and entrails; with a groan it staggered quivering to its feet, made a step forwards, trod on its own trailing, bleeding insides, fell again, groaning with anguish, quivering convulsively.

The people were delighted. They shouted and screamed and stood up on their seats and waved their kerchiefs, especially the women!

The picador, who picked himself up unhurt—indeed, cased in armour, he could not well be otherwise—was cheered and cheered, and bowed and smiled and took off his cap and swept it to the ground. And the band crashed loudly to drown the terrible groaning of the dying horse, struggling in agony on the sand. The bull, sorry rather than otherwise apparently, walked away to another part of the ring, tossing his head in pain as the blood dripped from it.

The people clapped delightedly. Suzee seeing all the women about her doing so, put up her little hands and clapped too.

I bent towards her and caught them and held them down in her lap.

"Be quiet," I said; "I won't have you clap such a disgusting sight."

She stopped at once. A Mexican woman on my other hand, looked daggers at me for an instant, divining my words, but she was too eager to see all the blood and the anguish in the arena, not to miss a throe of the dying horse, to turn her eyes away for more than a moment.

So, after a scowl at me, she directed them again, bulging with satisfaction, on the scene before her.

From then on, for about an hour, the same hideous thing went on; horse after horse was brought forward, pushed on the horns of the bull, torn and mangled beneath its cowardly rider, and then, if completely ripped open, dragged dead or dying from the ring; if its wound was not large enough to cause instant death, stuff or straw was thrust into it by the attendants and the dying animal kicked, lashed, and dragged to its feet to be thrown again on to the sharp horns amidst the shouts and laughs of the delighted crowd.

Once, in a general mêlée, when the bull and several picadors were in a tangled mass at one side of the ring, I saw one of these horses, terribly wounded, with its life pouring from it, emerge from the conflict and stagger unnoticed to the hoarding.

It came close to the wall of the ring and looked over; its glazed, anguished eyes gazed from side to side as if asking: "Is there no escape, no mercy anywhere?"

A spectator on the audience side of the hoarding raised his hand and struck it between the eyes. It tottered, staggered, and sank within the ring.

Eight horses had now been rendered useless, the arena was black and red with blood, in spite of the assiduous sprinkling of fresh sand, and there was a pause in the entertainment. The picadors had had their turn, the banderilleros were ready to appear, but the people were thoroughly enjoying themselves now and they stamped and roared "Caballos" till they were hoarse. That horrid cry for more and more horses to be produced that alarms the administrador, or manager, of the bull-fight.

In vain the attendants lashed and goaded the dying horses in the arena. They could not get them to their feet again. There is a limit to man's sway, the tortured life at last escapes him. The bodies were dragged away, more sand, and then the administrador himself, pale as ashes, stepped out before the audience howling for more blood.

"Señors," he commenced, "it is impossible to supply more than eight horses for one bull; there are five more bulls to be dispatched. They are more savage than this one. I must keep horses for them. Let the señors be reasonable and allow the show to continue."

At this promise of five more bulls there was general applause. The band rolled out fresh music. There was a thunder of drums and the banderilleros came on, gorgeous in velvet, glittering in spangle and tinsel.

The bull is weary now and has lost much of his blood; as from the first, he only longs to escape from this ring, and the mad monkeys who are gibing and gibbering at him in it. They came forward with their fresh weapons, shafts and arrows of iron decked up with coloured ribbons, which they throw at him and which stick on his shoulders and in his sides, drawing streams of blood wherever they strike him.

Maddened by those, he rushes at the flaming coats the men trail before his eyes; but the cruel little, dancing, monkey-like man with the cloak darts away before he can be touched, and at last, after repeated rushes and repeated failures, the grand creature stands still, wearied and disdainful, his head erect, the blood flowing from his wounds in which the darts move, swaying to and fro each time he stirs, causing him an agony he cannot understand. So he faces the great crowded ring contemptuously, and the people shout at him and call him a coward and scream for the espada to come and dispatch him.

The banderilleros retire: they have weakened the bull so that there is now no danger for the puny little two-legged creature who struts in next with a sword, and who is greeted with plaudits and triumphal music. Flowers are thrown him, bouquets, the men call him hero, the women throw kisses to him.

He bows to the President, then turns towards the

bull who stands erect still, though the loss of blood must be telling upon him, stands with that same air of deadly *ennui*, of weary scorn of all this folly which he has possessed from the first. Dusty and blood-stained his glossy coat, bloodshot his great lustrous eyes. As he looks round the circle already growing dim to them, does he long for his green Andalusian pastures, does he see again those pleasant streams by which his herd is wandering?

The little manikin sidles up and jabs him behind the shoulder with his sword. The bull turns upon him, and he runs for his life. But the bull does not deign to follow. With a great show of precaution where there is really no danger, the little man with the sword approaches again. Amidst cheers from the onlookers he plunges his sword between the shoulders of the dying monarch and then rushes backwards. The great beast sways, shivers in mortal anguish for a moment, and then without a sound sinks, for the first time in this cruel and unequal combat, to his knees. Sinks, full of a superb dignity to the end, and one asks oneself—"What *can* the scheme of creation be that gives a creature so clean-souled, so grand, into the power of such a miserable mass of vile lusts as man?"

A moment more and the head crowned with its tapering crescent horns sinks forwards. A gush of blood from the nostrils on the sand, and it is over. The glossy form is still—at peace.

With ridiculous manœuvres the little man comes up again to the great beast, obviously dead and harmless, and withdraws his sword which he waves triumphantly before the applauding populace.

While he capers about before his delighted admirers, the attendants come in and draw away with some difficulty the magnificent form of the slaughtered bull.

The music broke into a loud march. There was an interval of relaxation for the audience, to move, look about, chatter, and take refreshments.

"This is the end," I said to Suzee; "let us go now."

"Oh, but Treevor, that man said he had five more bulls, look, nobody is going yet," she returned, having evidently followed in her own sharp way the sense of the Spanish speech of the administrador.

"Do you want to see any more?" I asked. "I think it is dull and tedious, as well as horrible."

"The killing is not nice," she said, in deference to my opinions, I suppose; "but the music and the people are fun, I think. Do let us stay for one more fight. You won't want to bring me again."

"No, I certainly shan't," I answered.

"Then do let me stay now, Treevor, just one more time."

I shrugged my shoulders and sat back in my seat, and

after a second the little door opposite opened and another bull, this time apparently mad with pain, dashed into the ring.

The people applauded him and the shouts and clappings increased his excitement.

He bounded at full gallop across the sandy space and charged the hoarding that hemmed him in.

The audience were delighted, but the toreadors entered the ring and stood together at one side, looking anxious, and some of the attendants came up and received orders from them.

From the first the animal was unmanageable, out of all control. The goading and the enraging that goes on in the dens behind the arena had been overdone apparently, for the bull, wild with rage and pain, galloped madly round, taking no notice of the pallid group of toreadors.

At last one or two came forward with their cloaks of scarlet; the bull made a dash at them, scattering them on either side, then bounded on and with one tremendous leap cleared the hoarding that separates spectators from the rings, and landed bellowing in the corridor that ran round it just below our seats. It was full of onlookers drawn nearer than usual to the hoarding by the excitement, and they scattered and fled in all directions, while shriek upon shriek went up from the women all round us as they saw the bull clear the hoarding and come down amongst them.

With one accord they stood up. Like a great wave breaking, they rushed upwards to the highest part of the ring, shrieks and screams on every side telling of the trampled children and injured women in the frantic panic.

Suzee rose with the rest, livid and trembling, and would have rushed after that seething mass behind us, if I had not seized her arm and forced her back to her seat.

"Sit down, stay where you are," I said; "the bull will do you less harm than that trampling horde."

We were left there alone; groans and cries came from the panic-stricken, struggling mass of people behind us; just beneath us in the emptied corridor stood the bull, snorting with lowered head, pawing the ground; in the arena, the administrador, green with terror and anxiety, shouted commands to the pallid and trembling attendants.

I sat still, holding Suzee. The bull paused for a moment in front of us, then with his head lowered almost to the ground, made a terrific rush forwards, shattering the woodwork of the platform at our feet to atoms with his horns. Suzee gave a piercing shriek and fell across me, unconscious. The animal, startled by the scream, raised its head.

FIVE NIGHTS

In its rolling eyes I saw nothing but the madness of pain and terror. As it drew back for a second charge, in its mad effort to dash through the woodwork to liberty, I slipped sideways with the dead weight of Suzee on my arm, into the seats on one side. It was not an instant too soon. The next, the bull rushed forwards and our seats were falling in splinters about his head. Along, sideways, over chair after chair, I slipped, dragging and supporting Suzee as best I could. I heard screams of terror and suffering all round us as the panic spread amongst the people and they forced themselves in an ever-increasing mass upwards, fighting their way to the exits at the top of the ring.

My mind was made up. All before me was clear and open, the seats deserted, below me ran the corridor leading to the entrance by which we had come in. For that I would make.

There was some slight risk, for the bull, tired now of his futile efforts to destroy the wooden barriers in front of him, had turned back into the corridor and started on a mad gallop down it round the ring.

I must drop down into the corridor before I could arrive at the entrance, and unless he were stopped he might meet us in the corridor before I could reach the exit. But his arc of the circle was a long one, mine to the exit was short, and, anyway, I preferred to chance meeting him to trusting myself to the mercies of my own kind.

I leapt down into the passage, and, lifting Suzee into my arms, passed on rapidly to the wicket.

There was no one there. I went through, out into the golden sunlight.

Outside, the accident and the panic had not yet become known. I saw a carriage, with its driver asleep upon the box, close to the main gate. I went up to it, put Suzee in and spoke to the man.

"The lady has fainted," I said; "drive us back to the Hotel Iturbide."

The man, delighted at securing a fare so soon, seized the whip and reins and drove away full tilt before one of the struggling wretches in the bull-ring had succeeded in getting out.

Suzee recovered consciousness just before we reached the hotel, but when she had opened her eyes she closed them again instantly and covered her face with her hands with a cry of terror.

"Oh, Treevor, that awful bull; where is it now? It can't get at us, can it?"

"No, poor brute," I answered. "You are safe enough now, Suzee; you are miles away from the bull-ring."

She was trembling so much she could hardly walk up the stairs to our room, and when we got there I made her go to bed while I sat by her putting cold compresses on her head. She complained of such pain in it, I was afraid that the fright and shock would do her serious harm.

I sat up with her through the night, and towards morning she fell into a tranquil sleep.

I paced up and down the quiet room lighted only by the night light, thinking over the horrid scene of the afternoon, and when it grew to be day I was hungering so for a companion to speak to and to feel with me, that I drew out my writing-case and wrote a long letter to Viola.

CHAPTER XI

THE WAY OF THE GODS

"But, Treevor, I am so very dull when you go out, and when you are working it is as bad. I do miss my baby so to play with."

"You did not strike me as a very devoted mother when I saw you at Sitka," I answered.

"Oh, Treevor, he was a very fine boy, and I took so much care of him. Was he not a very large child?"

"Yes, he certainly was, and with a dreadful voice and a furious temper. It's no use worrying me, Suzee, about the matter. I dislike children very much, and I do not wish nor intend to have any of my own."

Suzee began to cry in the easy way she had. She seemed able to commence and leave off just when she chose.

"You are a little goose," I said jestingly. "You don't know when you are well off. For months and months you would be ill and disfigured, unable to come about with me or be my companion, unable to sit to me for my painting, and afterwards the child would be an unendurable tie and burden. Besides, as I say, I have an intense dislike to children and could never live with one anywhere near me. I am afraid, if you want them, you must go away from me, to some one who has your views."

Suzee came over to where I was sitting and knelt beside my chair, clasping both hands round my arm.

"Treevor," she said, almost in a whisper, "you are so beautiful with your straight face, every line in it is so straight, quite straight; and your black hair and your dark eyes and your dark eyebrows. I want that for my baby. I want a son just like you; he must be just like you, and then I should be so happy."

As she spoke, the lines of a poetess flashed across me, indistinctly remembered—"beauty that women seek after . . . that they may give to the world again."

Was this the reason of woman's love of beauty in men? Ah, not with all women! Viola loved beauty, as I did, as all artists do, as they love their art, for itself alone.

I stroked her smooth shining hair, gently, and shook my head, smiling down upon her.

"Do you not value my love for you?" I asked.

"Oh yes, yes; you know I do."

"Well, then understand this: you would utterly and entirely lose it if you became a mother."

Suzee shrank away from me.

"But why, Treevor? Hop Lee was so pleased with me . . ."

"Men have different tastes. And it is well they have, or the world would be worse than it is. Some men like children and domesticity and sick-nursing and

childish companionship; I don't. I like health and
beauty, and love and intellect about me, and women
who are straight and slim and can inspire my pictures.
That's why, Suzee, and I don't see any reason why I
shouldn't gratify my tastes as they do theirs. There
are plenty of men in the world who like being fathers
of families; the world can well allow an artist to give
it his art instead."

"Oh yes, Treevor, of course; but I am so sorry. I
am so dull without a baby."

We were sitting together in a light balcony of one of
the hotels at Tampico, and the subject of our conversation was one which had come up many times between
us lately.

Some months had slipped by since the accident in
the bull-ring. Suzee had recovered from the shock
with a few day's rest and care, and as soon as she was
better we had started on a tour through the country
places of Mexico, and as it grew colder we had worked
downwards to the gulf of Vera Cruz in the Tierra
Caliente, or Hot Lands, and now were making a stay
here on the coast, caught by the beauty of palm and
sea and shore.

Suzee, though apparently she had all that most young
women covet, had been for some time restless and
dissatisfied, and the reason soon appeared in conversa-
tions like that of to-day.

"Come along," I said, getting up; "see what a lovely evening it is, let's go for a walk along the sea-shore."

Suzee looked round at the translucent green bell of the sky that hung over us, disapprovingly.

"It's always fine weather," she said, rather sulkily; "and there's nothing to see on that old shore."

"Nothing to see!" I exclaimed in sheer amazement. Then I stopped short, remembering her indifference to all I valued, and added: "There are most beautiful shells of every shape and colour, wouldn't you like to get some of those?"

Suzee's face brightened immediately. This idea took her fancy at once. It appealed to her keen love of material things. Beauty in air and sky was nothing to her; but something she could pick up and handle, become possessed of, like the shells, deeply interested her. She rose at once.

"I had better take a basket, Treevor," she said, "to carry them back in." And while she went to get it, I leant over the balcony-rail musing on that great difference in character between woman and woman, man and man. Humanity might almost be divided into those two great parts—those who love and live in ideas; and those who love, and are wholly concerned with, material things.

She came back in a moment with a basket swinging

in her hand. It had not seemed so necessary here in Mexico that she should dress in Western clothes, so she had gradually relapsed into her gaily coloured silks and embroidered muslins and Zouave jackets. This style of dressing suited the tropical climate, and the convenances of Europe and America were too far off for anything to matter much here. It gave her constant occupation, too, the making of her costumes; for she was marvellously quick and dexterous with her needle, and if I gave her the silks she fancied she made them into dainty forms and embroidered them with the greatest skill. As she came back now with her basket the light fell softly on her lilac silk, all worked with gold thread, and on her pretty bare head with its block of black shining hair.

We started for the shore, Suzee all animation now and chattering on the possibility of sewing sea-shells into gold tissue or muslin.

The sky all round and overhead was palest green and strangely luminous, the sea before us stretched to the far horizon in tones of gentlest mauve and violet, beneath our feet was the firm brown sand for miles and miles unrolled like a glossy, sepia carpet. On one side broke the tiny waves in undulating lines of white; on the other, the wild sand-dunes, grown over with rough grass and waving cocoanut palms, came down towards the sea.

We walked on, both contented. I, in the strange colouring and the warm salt breath in the air, that stirred the palm leaves till they tossed joyfully in it; she, in the absorbing pursuit of the shells which lay along the sand, positively studding it, like jewels, with colour. The tide had recently gone down over the shore where we walked and left them radiant, gleaming with moisture in the low light of the sun, pink and scarlet, deepest purple and gold. She ran ahead of me, picking them up and filling her basket rapidly. I walked on slowly, thinking, while my eyes wandered over that shining, palpitating, gently heaving violet sea. She had given herself to me entirely—and what beauty she had to give! And yet she had failed to chain me to her in any way, greatly though she pleased my senses. It is, after all, something in the soul of a woman, in her inner self, that has the power of throwing an anchor into our soul and holding it captive. Mere beauty throws its anchor into the flesh, and after a time the flesh gives way.

In a little while Suzee came running back to me; her basket was full to overflowing: she was quite happy.

"Take me up in your arms and kiss me," she said. "Look, Treevor, we are all alone. What a great, great beach it is here, with not another soul to see anywhere."

As she said, the firm brown plain of glistening sand stretched behind us and before us with not another footfall to disturb its silence, the wide white sand-dunes were deserted, the palms tossed their greeting to the sea through the glory of calm evening light.

"Let us lie under those palms now; I am tired," she said as I kissed her. And we went together and lay down under the palms on a ragged tussock of grass, and the light fell and grew deeper in tone round us and the amethystine sea, flushed with colour, swayed and heaved, murmuring its low eternal song by our side.

A great vulture flapped heavily by and perched on a sand-hill not far from us, eyeing us somewhat askance, and some sea-gulls circled over us—otherwise we were undisturbed.

The following day we planned to come down the river Tamesi, which flows out at Tampico. We could not go up by boat, as the river was in flood and nothing could make headway against it, but the natives were adepts at steering a boat down with the rapid current, and knew how to handle it on the top of the flood.

We took the train some distance up the line, and alighted at a place where the river flowed by between high banks and where boats could be had from the villagers.

It was a perfect, cloudless day, and we reached our destination in the sweet fresh early hours of the morning. A walk through the tiny Mexican village brought us to the bank of the river where the Tamesi flowed by, heavily, grandly, in all the majesty of its flood.

The waters were brown and discoloured, but the sun glinting on its ripples turned them into gold, and the tamarisk on the bank drooped over it, letting its long strands float on the gliding water.

A little way down the bank, moored to the side, rocked a boat, of which the outline delighted me, and, to Suzee's annoyance, I stood still and drew out my note-book to make a sketch of it.

It appeared to be the larger half of one immense tree of which the inside had all been hollowed out, both ends were raised and pointed and, in the centre, four bent bamboo poles, inclined together, supported a finely plaited wicker-work screen, which shielded a patch about two yards square in the boat from the burning rays of the sun.

I finished the sketch in a few minutes, and we went on towards the boat; its owners, two Mexican Indians, were sitting on the bank engaged in mending one of their paddles. They were quite naked except for their loin cloths, and their bare, brown crouching figures gave the last touch of suggested savagery to the scene. The red, earthy banks of the river stretched before us desolate and sunburnt; the swollen, muddy river itself rolled swiftly and heavily along, silent, impressive; the dug-out, looking like a craft of primeval times, rocked and swayed noiselessly on the flood; the naked savages crouched over their broken paddle beneath the waving tamarisk; the sunlight fell torrid, blighting in its scorching heat, over all. The scene, with its rough, fresh, vigorous barbarism, delighted me. I slackèned my pace and stood still again before disturbing or interrupting the men.

"Suzee," I said suddenly, "I admire this picture before us immensely. I should like to see it in the Academy to cheer up jaded Londoners next season. I should be glad to stop here to-day to paint it. We can go down the river to-morrow."

Suzee stared at me in dismay.

"Oh, Treevor, you don't want to stay here all day, do you? It's so hot, and there's nothing to do, and, we shall miss the fair at Tampico to-night. You promised we should see it."

I sighed. It was true, I had said something about the fair, but I had forgotten it. Suzee, however, never forgot things of this sort and she radically objected to any change being made in a programme. She did not adapt herself quickly and easily to changed moods or circumstances.

Had Viola been with me, she would have said at once:

"*Would* you like to stay here instead of going on? Do let's stay, then. We can go down the river any time." And had I suggested there would be nothing for her to do, she would have answered:

"Oh yes, I shall enjoy sitting watching you." Her interest had always lain in me, in her companion; to what we did she was indifferent; provided we were together and I was pleased, she was content. It is just this difference in women that makes it so delightful to live with some, so impossible to live with others. There are some, very few, of whom Viola was one, who delight in the society of the man they love, who drink in pleasure for themselves from his enjoyment; there are others, like Suzee, the majority, who are always at conflict with his wishes in little things, striving after some independent aim or project.

And they wonder why, after a time, their companionship grows irksome and they are deserted. They also wonder why sometimes the other woman is adored and worshipped and grows into the inner life of a man till he cannot exist without her.

I felt then an extraordinary longing to be free from Suzee, to be alone. Here was a picture, set ready to my hand. A scene we had come upon accidentally and that, in its barbaric simplicity, was not easily to be found again. It was strong, striking, original. I saw it before my mind's eyes on the canvas already, with "On the Tamesi, Mexico" written on the margin.

How could she ask me to lose it? But I could not break my word, as she chose to keep me to it.

I said nothing, and, after a pause of keen disappointment, I walked slowly on again towards the boat.

The men were Indians, but they understood a little Spanish and I bargained with them to take us down to Tampico where we should arrive about seven the same evening, in time for the fruit-market and general fair held in the Plaza.

They were glad enough to take us as they were going down in any case with a load of bananas and our fares would pay them well for the extra space we took up in the boat.

They hauled the dug-out to the bank and jumped in, clearing it of old fruit baskets and arranging some rugs and mats under the shade of the wicker screen. Behind that, to the stern, the boat was filled with the rich yellow of the bananas, the ruddy pink of the plantains, and mellow, translucent orange of the mangoes. They lay there in great heaps, leaving only just space enough for the stern paddler to stand.

The men motioned us to get in, which we did, and took our seats cross-legged in the centre on the mats, beneath the awning; glad of its shade, for the sun's rays grew fiercer every moment.

I put my unused sketch-pad behind me, gazing back regretfully over the yellow flood. The men pushed the boat out on to the waters and sprang in themselves each armed with a long paddle; one taking his stand in front of us, one at the stern, and directed our little craft to the centre of the huge and sullen stream. It rolled from side to side as it shot out over the surface, but as soon as the men got their paddles to work, evenly with long alternate strokes, the flood bore us along, swiftly, smoothly, the dug-out floating steadily without rocking.

The men stood, alert and watchful, on the lookout for submerged trees and floating débris; for at the swift rate we were now floating, any collision would have brought great danger.

I leant back, watching the banks pass swiftly by, mile upon mile of red earth and waving tamarisk under the scorching blue. Suzee seemed more interested in the stalwart figure of our forward boatman and the play of his fine muscles under the smooth brown skin of his shoulders where the sun struck them.

Had I loved her more I should have been angry; as it was, I was only amused, and glad of anything that occupied her attention and relieved me of the necessity of listening and replying to her childish chatter.

How fast the boat sped on over the surface of the whirling stream that rushed by those red banks, swift as the flash of life, hurrying on to lose itself in the ocean as life hurries on to lose itself in the infinite.

The banks were getting flatter, here and there the

stream widened, the wild tamarisk, child of the desert, disappeared and gave way to cultivated fields and wide tracts of the maguey plant, dear and valuable to the Mexican as the date-palm to the East-Indian. Rough yellow adobe huts stood here and there, their crude colouring of unbaked mud turned into gold by that great painter, the tropical sun; and sometimes a palm stood by a hut, cutting the fierce light blue of the sky with its delicate, fine, curved, drooping branches; sometimes the dark, glossy green of the organ cactus rose like jade pillars beside it. All these sped by us quickly, though at times the scene was so engaging I could have held it with my eyes; but ruthlessly we were whirled forward and the scenes on the bank kept slipping behind us, just as our dearest scenes and incidents in life keep slipping past, swallowed up by the ever-pursuing distance.

Our red banks had been growing flatter and flatter and now they seemed to disappear, and the river instantly broadened itself out and spread into a lake, as if glad of the expansion. Over each bank, far on either side, it rolled itself out in great shining flats of water, glittering and dazzling, impossible to look at in this hour of noon; and as if tranquillity had come to it with its greater freedom, the river flowed more slowly and gently.

Our boatmen stood at ease at their paddles, pushing

306

quietly along, and I looked round with interest. We were in the centre of a great lake in which here and there submerged trees and bushes made green islands. An endless lake it seemed, a great waste of gleaming water. We floated along gently like this for some time, and then almost suddenly when I looked ahead, I saw the end of the lake was closing in, there were woods and forests now upon its margin; a few more strokes of the paddle and we were in shade, heavy, cool shade, where the water gleamed with a bronze shimmer. Narrower still the lake end became, the margins drew together, and with a swift push forwards, like the bolt of a rabbit to its hole, our boat shot forwards into a little tunnel of darkness before us over which the interlacing boughs of the trees made a perfect arch. We were in the forest, and it was dark and cool as it had been brilliant, dazzling with light and heat, on the lake. A dim, green twilight reigned here, and the river went with a swift, dark rush, past the roots of the overhanging trees. How they stooped over the water! Swinging down, interlacing boughs from which vine and flowering creeper trailed. The standing figure of the boatman had to bend down and sway from side to side to avoid the clinging wreaths or mossy boughs and be wary with his paddle to escape the snags projecting from the banks.

How grand the great spanning arches of the trees

were, above our heads! Finer than any cathedral roof wrought by man. How soft the luminous green twilight seemed in the long aisle! And constantly from bough to bough twined a great scarlet-flowered creeper, glowing redly in all this mystery of shade. The banks were thick with vegetation, one thing growing over another, with tropical luxuriance, until sometimes here and there groups of plants, weary with the struggle each to assert itself, had all fallen together over the bank and trailed their long strands wearily in the water.

The stream zigzagged on before us, here darkly green to blackness; there, where the light pierced through the upper boughs, a golden bronze; then blue and silver where it caught and eddied and played round a fallen tree or a stump in the river bed.

We were going fast now, and as we shot along the glimmering stream we left the thick green part of the forest behind us. The river broadened out, expanded widely on either side, and in a few more minutes we seemed on a chain of infinite lakes spreading out on every side under and through the trees, which, though they met far overhead forming a perfect and continuous roof, were bare of leaves and flowering vines beneath. Grey trunks and bare brown branches in bewildering numbers now surrounded us, and the sheets of water reflected all so perfectly down to infinite

depths that one lost sense of reality. Boughs and branches, all arching and curving and spreading above us in
the softened light, and boughs and branches and inverted
trees below us, arches and curves and twisted networks;
between, those long gleaming flats of water on which
we floated silently without sense of motion, ever onwards.

"It is a little like the wood at Sitka in times of river
flood," Suzee said to me, as we sat together watching
the mirrored stems and branches glide by beneath our
boat.

"Yes?" I answered, smiling back upon her at the
remembrance of the wood.

The stream was a wide flat here, and our boatmen
suddenly directed the boat to the bank and brought
it to a standstill. "We want to go on land here and
buy mangoes," he explained in Spanish.

"Very good mangoes can be got here."

We looked round and saw, some distance from the
margin, amongst the stems of the trees standing
thickly together, an adobe building, low and flat, and
some figures, not much more clothed than our boatmen,
squatting in front of it, counting mangoes from a great
pile into baskets.

He fastened the dug-out to one of the many tree
stems, drawing it close to the bank, and then he and
his companion landed, leaving us alone in the lightly
swaying boat.

"We'll have lunch here, Suzee, don't you think?" I asked her, beginning to unpack the small basket we had brought. "Can you make tea for us there, do you think?"

"Oh yes, quite easily; they have a little kitchen here."

In the forepart of the boat the Indians had fixed a piece of tin with a few bricks round it, forming a hearthstone and stove. On this they cooked their own food as their surrounding pots and kettles shewed. A few embers from their last cooking glowed still between the bricks. Suzee leant over them, blew them into a blaze and then set our kettle on, getting out her little cups and saucers and ranging them on the floor of the boat.

I sat back and watched her. The whole scene was a delightful one and rivalled the one I had noted at starting. The gleaming water spread itself in large flat mirrors on every side, and the trees standing in it reflected beneath, and reaching up to the lofty roof of overarching, interlaced boughs above us, gave the effect of a hall of a thousand columns. The adobe house of the fruit-seller seemed standing on a precarious island, so high had the floods risen round it, and numerous empty baskets and crates, evidently lifted from their moorings on the bank, drifted slowly about on the silvery tide. Our boat itself was a lovely object with its fairy lines, its thread of smoke going up from it, and the little Oriental figure bending over the red embers in its prow.

We lunched and had our tea in this cool retreat of softened light, and knew the sun was beating with its murderous noonday glare just without. The boatmen came back after an interval with a huge load of mangoes which they piled into the boat, and offered us sixty for five cents. I gave them the five cents and took two or three of the fruits for myself and Suzee. Then the moorings were undone, the men jumped in, and paddled us swiftly onwards. The proprietor of the adobe hut came to the edge of his grove and saluted, as we passed by on a rapid current; then he and hut and mangoes all glided from us, quickly as a dream, and we were borne forward through the wonderful maze of trees over the tranquil sheets of water.

All through the golden Mexican afternoon we descended the river, down, ever downwards, to the sea. Sometimes in the deep green shadows of overhanging trees, passing through the heart of a forest; sometimes out in the burning open beneath the clear blue of the sky, between flat plains of open country; sometimes on the breast of wide lakes; sometimes between high banks, where the boat went dizzily fast and the waters passed the paddles with a sharp hiss as we rushed on; and each of those moments was a delight to me, and even Suzee seemed affected by the beauty and the poetry of the river, for she leant against me silent and absorbed and her eyes grew soft and dreaming as the visions on the golden banks swept by; fields of sugar-cane and maguey, coffee plantations with their million scarlet berries, waving banana and palm, masses of delicate bamboo rustling as the warm breeze stirred them.

As the day melted into evening, the sky flushed a deep rosy red and seemed to hang over us like a great hollowed-out ruby glowing with crimson fires. The waterway of the river before us turned crimson, and all the ripples in it were edged and flecked with gold. The great lagoons, when we passed through them now, reflected the peace of the painted skies and the marsh lilies floating on their surface became jewels set in gold as the water eddied round them.

In half an hour the glory faded, leaving a transparent lilac sky over which the darkness closed with all the swiftness of the tropics.

As we neared the sea and the warm salt breath came up to us we saw the light over the Market Square in Tampico and the masses of soft shadow of the trees in the Plaza.

Frail, wooden boat-houses, with shaky landing-stages built out over the water, lined the banks on either side, and at one of them our boatmen suddenly drew in, and we disembarked in the soft darkness, suffused with the red light from the square and vibrating with the music from a band playing there behind the trees.

We got out and walked along the river-bank towards the seashore, where the sea lay calm and still, its black, gently heaving surface reflecting the light of the stars. Where the river debouched, there was a sheltered cove of fine white sand, and here every species of gaily painted craft was drawn up. The light from the Market Square, ablaze with lamps, reached out to it and shewed boat after boat of fantastic shape and colour, with striped awnings fixed on bamboo poles over their centre, lying in the shelter of the palm-trees that fringed the cove. We rounded the slight promontory on our left hand and came full into the light of the animated town.

The fair was in progress, and numbers of fruit-sellers from all the country round, from the adobe hut and the large hacienda, or estate, of the Mexican gentleman, alike, had brought down their load of fruit to sell in Tampico.

Not only was the Plaza itself filled to overflowing with fruit and other stalls, but they reached down almost to the shore, and very rich and Oriental the scene looked, framed in deepest shadow from the Plaza trees on one side, and the smooth, black, starlit darkness of the sea on the other.

Each stall had its own light, a bowl of flaming naph-

tha mounted on a bamboo pole, and the light fell over
the golden fruit—mangoe, plantain, and banana piled
high upon it, and also all round the vender's feet as
he stood by his stall in town costume of one long white
muslin robe.

There were other stalls where they sold Mexican
drawn-work, carved leather and filigree silver, others
again with chairs set round where one could have iced-
fruit drinks or coffee, and the band played sonorously
and the crowd, good-natured, laughing, gaily dressed,
men, women, and children of all sizes, strolled amongst
the stalls, buying, looking, chattering, flirting, in the
soft, damp heat of the night.

Suzee was enchanted and stared about her with
bold, lustrous glances, pleased at the admiring looks
of the men on her strange pretty face. She steered me
up to the silver-filigree stall and there had all the vender's wares put out for her inspection. She was keen
enough where her own particular interests were concerned, and the sellers of artificial jewellery tempted
her with their sparkling gewgaws not at all. Real
solid worth was what she intended to obtain, and her
taste in choosing the silver was excellent.

Would I buy her this? Would I buy her that?
And I assented to everything. I only wished I could
buy myself pleasure as easily.

She chose a necklet, a brooch, and numberless

bangles for her arms, all the smallest she could find, those generally made for children. When these loaded her little arms and the necklet was clasped round her throat she was happy, and the curious, interested Mexicans gathered in a little knot round us, looked on with interest and evident approval at the Englishman's money being spent amongst them.

We stayed in the square buying to her heart's content till eleven, and then, after supper at a little table beneath the Plaza trees where the band played loudest, for Suzee loved music when it meant noise, we went back to the hotel and to bed.

The next day I went by train to the place where we had embarked for our voyage down the Tamesi, fully equipped with my materials for a sketch—and alone.

Suzee, adhering to her idea that it would be dull and hot on the river-bank, had preferred to stay in the hotel playing with some of the treasures bought yesterday at the fair.

Alone and undisturbed I sat all day sketching, till the fires were lighted in the West and warned me I must turn homewards. I had a good picture, and I packed up my traps with that deep sense of satisfaction that accomplished work alone can give and walked slowly to the station. As my thoughts slipped on to Suzee a sense of anxiety came over me. Time was going on. The year would soon be over. What did I intend to do? Once the year was past it would be impossible for me to continue living with her, even for a day. And now I felt so often I would rather be alone than with her. How would she feel over our separation? How could I provide for her happiness when I took back my freedom?

Satiety was beginning to creep over the passion I had for her, and that was still farther checked now that I knew she looked upon it more as a means to an end— the child—rather than enjoyed it for itself.

It worried me greatly this thought of her future and how I was going to provide for it, and it seemed sometimes as if it might be better to give in to her; perhaps without me she would be happy if she had a child as she wished, provided I could make, as I could, a good allowance to both. But then even with a child I could not imagine Suzee would want to remain alone, and what would be the fate of a child if other lovers came, or a husband? . . .

While I did not think that Suzee loved me deeply, deep emotion not being within her range of powers, it was difficult to see how I could find for her an existence as pleasant as she led with me.

All these things worried me greatly, and as Fate willed it, needlessly.

How often in this life a way is suddenly opened out through circumstances where we least expect it.

The Greeks said—"For these unknown matters a god shall find out the way." And often indeed it happens that Fate steps in, and in some way our wildest dreams have never pictured turns all our life to another hue suddenly before our eyes.

One night when I had been making a little head of Suzee in her prettiest mood on my canvas, she came and sat on my knee and begged me to give her, as a reward for her sitting, a narrow band of gold I always wore on my left arm above the elbow.

I refused, for Viola had given it to me and locked it on my arm. She had the key and I, even had I wished, could only have had it taken off by means of another key or melting the gold.

At my refusal there was a storm of tears as usual, but it soon passed over on my kissing her and promising we would go to a jeweller's on the morrow and have one something like it put on her own arm.

She soon fell asleep after peace was restored, but I lay awake for hours watching the tracery of palm shadows on the wall opposite, thrown there by the light of the square. At midnight the lamp was put out, the room grew black, without a ray of light, and after a time I, too, fell asleep.

I was awakened by a curious sense of a presence in the room. My eyelids flew open, my ears strained. The room was one solid block of blackness, there was no ray of light anywhere. I could see and hear nothing for a moment, though I was certain another living thing had entered the room. Then at the same instant there was a violent vibration of the bed beneath me and a piercing scream from Suzee, a blind, wild cry to me for protection.

Instinctively I threw my arms out to her. Her body was struggling, writhing. I felt it as my hands shot out and gripped fiercely, in the thick darkness, round two hard hairy arms, tense, rigid, as they held her down.

Suzee's voice broke out suddenly as my grip possibly loosened the pressure of those other hands upon her throat, and she was speaking in *Chinese*. A hot breath came on my eyes, some face must have been close to mine in the blackness; under my arms, on Suzee's wildly heaving body, I felt something moving, warm and slow and soft, and knew that it was blood.

"Suzee," I called to her across her clamour of terrified entreaty, "get a light if you can."

The hot breath came nearer.

"Devil! Devil! This is your promise, your English word." The sound came to me like the hiss of steam close to my ear, but I knew the voice of Hop Lee —Hop Lee buried in Sitka, thousands of miles away.

The arms in my clutch struggled furiously; in their spasm of muscular effort they tore me upwards from the bed, as the lock of my fingers would not give way.

Suzee's voice clamoured in passionate entreaty, unintelligible to me. Then suddenly came a terrific twist, which wrenched away one of the arms, and a lightning stab, a deep burning in my shoulder, and simultaneously a blaze of light. Over me hung the bent old form of Hop Lee, his right arm, lifted up, held a long knife raised for its second stab. His face was alight with fury. Scarlet was already running in bright ribands over the whiteness of the bed, Suzee's blood and my own. I threw up my left arm and caught his wrist and turned the hand and knife upwards till it pointed to the ceiling, my own arm stretched to the fullest length upright. Suzee gave one horrible cry of terror, animal terror, and then there was silence beside me.

"She has fainted, has fainted," my brain muttered in itself. A sickening fear came into it as silence fell after that one awful cry.

I had my revolver under my pillow. If I could reach it! I looked up to the small red eyeballs of the Chinaman.

They were insane, glaring, full of the wild, unreasoning lust to kill. Some instinct moved me to speak.

"You were dead, I heard. I never had your wife while you were alive."

"Liar! Liar! You shall pay me in blood."

His hand with the knife in it twisted itself round in my grip. I felt my uplifted arm losing its force. What was draining my strength? That stream coming softly from my shoulder.

I lifted myself, trying to throw him backwards. My arm suddenly bent at the elbow and his hand with the knife in it zigzagged downwards very near to my throat. Age and feebleness had disappeared from him. He was strong now with the strength of insanity and of that blind leaping fury that glared out of his distorted face. There was a sudden struggle as he dropped on my chest, then with my hand still locked on his wrist we rolled together onto the floor.

A moment and we were up on our feet and he had forced me backwards to the bed. I felt my strength was going, but I still clung with a steel-like clutch to his wrist and kept the pointed knife at bay. As he bent me backwards on to the bed near the pillow, I took my right hand from his arm, snatched the revolver from under the pillow, thrust it into his face between the eyes, and fired.

He fell forwards, a great hole torn in his forehead, from which a river of blood poured, joining the bright ribands and with them making a sea of crimson.

I looked across him to where Suzee lay motionless.

"Suzee," I said, my breath almost dying in my throat.

She stirred slightly. I was beside her in a moment. Her eyelids opened slowly. Then her eyes filled with terror.

"Where is he?" she muttered.

"Dead; he cannot hurt you any more. You are safe now."

"No, Treevor, I am dying; it pains me so here."

She laid one hand on her breast and I saw the blood well up between two fingers. I tore aside the muslin veils on her bosom and found the wound: it was not large, just one clean stab, turning purple at the edges.

"It is deep, Treevor; so deep. And it bleeds inside me. It is drinking my life. I have only a few minutes to tell you. Hold up my head. I can't breathe."

I slipped my arm beneath her little neck. My heart seemed breaking with distress; black tides of resentment, of rage went through me, that she should be torn from me.

"Listen, Treevor. It was I that lied to you. I told you he was dead, and the child. They were not. I ran away. I left them at Sitka. I came to 'Frisco and took refuge with that woman. Then I wrote to you."

A sudden horror of her seemed to enfold me as I heard.

How she had lied and deceived me! And forced me to break my word!

"Because I wanted you so much and I knew you

would never have me if you thought he was still alive.
. . . Your stupid promise. What are promises when
one loves? I wanted you, Treevor, so much! So
much!"

Some of the old fire flashed out of the dying eyes, a
hungry, despairing look.

"Kiss me, Treevor. Say you forgive me."

But I could not. For the moment I was so stunned,
so overwhelmed by this sudden revelation of her deception.

A deathly physical faintness was creeping over me;
a sensation like the beginning of long-denied sleep
which rolls at last like an unconquerable tide, obliterating everything, through the exhausted frame, was in-
vading my whole body. I clasped one hand mechanically round the bed-rail to support myself, the ground
seemed to lift and sway beneath my feet.

I looked down on the little oval face that had lived
so near to me through the last year. How pale it was
now, framed in the crimson mist that stretched across
the bed! At the slight, exquisite body so often held in
my arms. Was I to lose them now for all time?

"I did it all for you, because I wanted you so much.
Do kiss me and say you forgive. I shall not rest through
a thousand years if you will not."

Grey shadows were collecting in her face, some
unseen hand seemed drawing the eternal veil between

us. To me, life, with all its doings, was far away. I myself was standing in the uncertain mists of death. Wide, limitless, and grey, the great plains of the hereafter seemed opening before me, dim, silent, and mysterious.

Life, with its glare of colour, its triumphant music, its crash of sound, was far behind me, almost forgotten; like clouds of indefinable tint, piled up on some distant horizon, rose the memories of its loves, its woes, its crimes.

Her weak voice calling on me to forgive seemed to have little meaning to me now. I leant forward, clasping her dying body to me, and kissed her lips, murmuring some words of consolation. Then the grey mists rose up over my eyes sealing them, and I sank slowly into the perfect darkness.

PART FIVE

THE WHITE NIGHT

CHAPTER XII

THE FLAMES OF LIFE'S FURNACE

A LARGE room with open windows shewing a great square of hot blue sky and a palm branch that swayed in front of them, bright gold in the vivid light, was before my eyes as I lay alone, stretched out on my bed, the mosquito-curtains draped round me, and raised on the side next the windows.

How many weary days and nights had gone slowly by since that night which hung veiled in crimson mists in my memory! Horrible night of anger, of struggle, of death, of blood! Would its remembrance always cling to me like this?

Hop Lee thought I had broken my promise to him. That was the poisoned thorn that rankled and twisted and festered within me. No wonder he had cursed me and wanted to kill me. And Suzee—how well she had deceived me! I remembered her as she had sat trying to weep at the supper-table in San Francisco, telling me of the last moments of Hop Lee, her own devotion to him, and the child in their dying sufferings! Husband and child that she had deserted so gladly! A dull anger burnt within me at the thought of that deception, and most fiercely at the knowledge that she had forced me to break my word.

Yet that anger, strongly though it flamed against her, could not wholly dry the tears that came between my lids as I thought of her. She had loved me in her own selfish, childish way, and had risked her own life as well as mine to come to me.

After all, was it not I who had been in the wrong from the first? I had known she was married. Why had I ever looked at her with that admiration which had stirred her passion for me? Morley had warned me. Now it had ended like this and nearly cost us all our lives. But I, the most guilty of the three, had escaped, and they were both dead.

I appeared to have broken my promise, and now, after already injuring him so much—one who had never injured me—I had killed Hop Lee. I had taken his wife, who, he had said, was more than his life. Not satisfied with that, I had taken his life, too! How horrible it all was! I felt suffocated beneath the weight of it. But surely, surely it was Suzee who had thrown this burden on me? Yes, but I had begun the evil far back in the sunny days at Sitka.

Truly, as I had said to Morley, "One never knows in life."

I had killed him, a poor harmless, defenceless old man who had trusted me!

One thing after another had gradually pushed me on to this climax, all having their origin in those careless glances exchanged in the Sitka tea-shop.

They had thought I should die, too, all the people who had rushed into the room and found us that night. Myself unconscious, and the others dead.

The cold voice of a doctor had been the first I had heard as sense came back to me with the damp night air from the window blowing on my face:

"He's done for, I should say, you'd better take his depositions if he can speak."

I had opened my eyes and seen some men carrying out the body of Hop Lee and the tiny pliable form of dear little Suzee that I should never see or clasp again.

The landlord had come up ashy-pale and shaking, with a note-book in his hand, and had questioned and re-questioned me, and I had answered until I fainted again.

Next, after a black gap, I came to beneath the surgeon's probe which he was thrusting into my wound, as he would a fork into cold meat.

"He won't get through, I should think; he has too much fever," he was saying, in the regular callous professional voice.

"But I'm going to try the effect of this new antiseptic dressing, I want to see if it does harm or not."

I opened my eyes and looked up at his hard, thin-lipped face, and he seemed somewhat disconcerted; but only jabbed his probe in a little deeper and remarked jocularly:

"Ah, I see, you're tougher than I thought."

More oblivion, and when I next came to I knew that *they* had both been carried away from me and buried—Hop Lee, and his wife beside him, and that that chapter in my life was, for ever and ever, closed.

Now I was in charge of a hospital nurse. A horrible creature she was, lean and hard-faced, with a straight slit across her face for mouth, and little grey, cruel eyes. Like a nightmare she hung round my bed, preventing me from getting better.

All the fiendish tortures and cruelties that she had witnessed within the hospital walls had, I suppose, made her the thing she was.

Days had passed, and very slowly a little strength had crept back into me, enough for me to see I was not getting well as quickly as my youth and strength would let me if there were no drawback. I drew all my forces together to try and understand this, and then I noticed that regularly after each dose of physic I went back a little.

More fever, more pain in my shoulder, more delusions before the brain. Each morning when the vitality within me had struggled through the evil effects of my medicine I was better, then came the harpy-faced nurse to the pillow—my dose—then pain and illness again.

The look on the face of the woman as I drank it was extraordinary. A sly, pleased look, as one sees on the face of a schoolboy dismembering a living fly.

One day I took the glass as usual from her, but instead of raising it to my lips, turned it upside down through the window.

The woman turned red, and then livid.

"What does that mean, sir, may I ask?"

"Simply that I am not going to take any more medicine, thank you," I replied quietly, "as I now wish to get well."

"My orders from the doctor are that you shall take it," she said grimly; "and I'll make you."

She poured out another glass of the medicine and approached the bed, with the intention, it seemed, of opening my mouth and pouring it down. But I had had no weakening, sense-destroying drug that morning, and nature was rapidly curing me.

She forgot that. As she came up, I sprang from the bed, put my hand on her shoulder, and forced her to the door. She shrieked and protested, but she could not resist. I put her outside and locked the door.

Then I sank down trembling with exhaustion, for I was very weak. But I rejoiced to know my strength had come back even that much. I crossed to the win-

dow after a moment and looked out. In the distance
glimmered the sea, blue and joyous and beautiful.
How I longed to be out near it, in its warm salt breeze!
Beside my window grew the companion of my weary
hours, the waving palm; beneath there was a little
flagged court, shut in by small buildings belonging to
the hotel. There was a well there and a banana-tree,
and a man sitting down plucking alive a struggling fowl.
I called to him in Spanish:

"Send the administrador to me." And he looked up.

A frightened look came into his face as he saw who it
was that called him. Then he nodded, and carrying the
unhappy bird by its feet, head downwards, disappeared
into the hotel.

People and things move slowly with the Spaniards.
I waited an hour, gazing out into the amethystine distance, wondering if Suzee's glad, careless, irresponsible
little spirit was dancing there in the sunbeams; and
then a knock came at the door.

I walked to it and said: "Who is there?"

I recognised the voice of the administrador in his
answer, and unlocked the door and bid him come in.

He did so, with an alarmed aspect.

"Have you seen the nurse?" I asked.

"Yes," he replied; "she told me you were again
delirious and had refused to take your medicine, and
that she must refuse all responsibility for you."

"I am not at all delirious, as you see," I answered; "I simply want to get well, and each time I take their stuff I get worse; so I am going to cease taking it. Now what I ask you to do is to keep that woman and the doctor and the surgeon out of my room. All I want is to be left alone, to be quiet. The surgeon took all the stitches out yesterday. There is no need for *him* to see me again, and the others I won't have in here."

"But the responsibility, really, Señor," the man muttered looking all ways at once, "and the good doctor—such an amiable man. What object could he have in not curing the Señor quickly?"

"The object of prolonging his fees," I answered smiling, "I should think. When I get well, his fees stop." Then it occurred to me this man had also an object in keeping me here, since my hotel bill would certainly stop, like the doctors' fees, when I got well; so I added:

"What day of the month is it? The twentieth? Well, listen to this. If I am well, perfectly well by the end of the month, I will give you a cheque for fifty pounds in addition to my bills, just to show my goodwill."

Now £50 is much to a Mexican, and over this man's face spread a look as of one who has a glimpse of Paradise. He looked down immediately, however, and said deprecatingly:

"How can I influence the Señor's getting well? These things are as the good God wills. I can hire a Sister to pray for the Señor. That I can do."

"Thank you," I said. "But if you will keep the doctor and nurse out of my room and send me good food and water I shall get well and the fifty pounds is yours. Do you understand, if they come into this room again you lose it. I only wish to be alone."

The man bowed and bowed.

"As the Señor wishes, but the good amiable doctor, what should I say to him?"

"What you please, only don't let him come near me."

"And when the Señor is well there are many little matters to settle. The Consul and the Magistrate . . ."

I stopped him.

"Not now. I am to have ten days in peace, and alone, or you don't get the money."

The man stood bowing and shuffling and muttering for some minutes. Then the thought of the £50 came before him too dazzling to resist, and with a final: "It shall be exactly as the Señor wishes," he withdrew.

And so now I lay alone. Ah, what a comfort solitude is!

Freedom and solitude! Are these not two sweet Sisters of Mercy?

How few of all worldly ills and sorrows can they not either cure or assuage? Or, rather, perhaps, ought one not to call them mates, from which the child, Content, is born?

I lay there, weak and suffering still, but a balm seemed poured all over me, for now I was alone.

I fell asleep after a time and did not wake till it was dark. I felt stronger, better. Sleep had nursed me in her own way through all the afternoon.

A lamp had been lighted on the table beside me and only needed turning up. There was a tray of food there and a carafe of water. I took a little of both and felt life stirring in all my veins, now that the paralysing grip of the deadly drugs they had been giving me was lifted off.

I lay still, gazing about the large, shadowy room and into the violet dusk of the square beyond the window, and then gradually sleep came over me again.

In less than an hour I started up from my bed, wide-awake. I thought I had been with Hop Lee. I looked round the room. All was just as I had seen it last. I sank back on my pillow. "It was only a vivid dream," I said to myself, and then fell to wondering what the dream had been. I could not remember. It seemed some communication had been made to my brain while I slept, that it had received very clearly, but now that I was awake it could not retain nor understand it, but it could, and did remember that I had dreamed of Hop Lee, and that it was a pleasant dream.

332

Yes, the man I had murdered had been with me, had spoken to me, and the impression was that of rest, of calm, of some aching self-reproach being appeased.

"Just a dream, of course," I said to myself; "but how odd that I cannot remember at all what he said." An hour perhaps passed by while I lay quiet, strangely comforted by the dream I had forgotten; and then I lapsed back into sleep and again Hop Lee was with me, speaking, telling me something earnestly, exhorting me gently, and again I woke with a feeling of gratitude, of peace; but I could recall nothing of what had been said to me.

The light burned steadily beside me, and I sat up and thought.

The feeling of tranquillity that spread through me, so different from the feverish self-reproach that had gripped me ever since I had killed Hop Lee was so marked, so wonderful in its effect on me that I could not feel it was the result of a dream. No, the spirit of the old man had been there, absolving me of my broken word, absolving me of his murder. The fact that I could not remember, could not recall or understand when awake my dream or his words, seemed to shew that in sleep a mysterious message from a hidden source had been conveyed to me, which, from its nature and the nature of my ordinary material brain, could not be received by the latter. From that hour I began to get well rapidly. Often and often in the long nights or the lonely quiet days, I tried to call up a dream to me, a vision of either of them again; often I longed to speak to Suzee once more. But never again did any shade come to my pillow. He had come that once, of that I was convinced. To others it would always seem as if I had dreamed that night. I knew, by some inner sense, I had been spoken to by the soul of the old dead Chinaman, and forgiven.

The time passed evenly in that calm solitude. Sometimes still I was burnt with fever and racked with pain and got but poor food, and often longed for a hand to give me water in the dark nights. And I longed—ah, how I desired, infinitely, to send to Viola, tell her, and ask her to come to me!

I felt she would come then, that she would fly to me once she heard I was ill, in actual need of her.

But my pride refused to let me do this.

I had begged her to come in the name of our love, appealed to her through our passion. I would never appeal to her pity.

Besides, I could not bear that she should see me now, wrecked in strength, a shadow, a skeleton of myself.

Fever had reduced me to the last thin edge of existence. As I stretched out my arms before me, they looked like some grim ghastly stranger's, I did not recognise them. No, she should come back to me when

334

I had regained the full glory of my health and strength that I knew she delighted in.

So I waited with all the patience I could command, and sleep and Nature nursed me between them till I was quite well.

Then came long-drawn-out procedure in the Mexican courts. I had documents to write and sign, affidavits to make out, interrogations to answer; but finally the Law was satisfied. I was acquitted. I heard the decision with a curious feeling. How little it seemed to matter beside the inner knowledge of my heart, that Hop Lee himself had been with me, and knew and understood.

One afternoon then, after the satisfying of nearly endless claims upon me, I looked at the long, flat, rolling sea with its reefs of palms for the last time, and took the train northwards away from Tampico.

The year was not yet over, but I was going back to be in London, or very near it. For would she not write first to my club? and here it took at least three weeks for my letters sent on from the club to reach me.

I did not wish to live actually in town yet till Viola joined me, to advertise our separation, unnecessarily, to our friends, but I thought I would live practically hidden somewhere near, so that letters could reach me from London the same day.

Within a month I was back in London and went first of all to call for letters. Amongst them I recognised instantly there was not one from Viola. And, depressed and disappointed, I went down into the country, to work.

Work, the dear mistress of an artist's life, the one that never leaves him but is there always waiting to receive him back to her, to console him in her arms for all the wounds that love has made.

Month after month went by and I worked at the painting, turning into finished pictures the many sketches life with Suzee had given me.

As I worked on some of these a wave of sad reflection would sweep over me, of memory of her, but the recollection of the deceit and lies in which her love for me had been always cloaked came with that memory and blunted the poignant edge of it.

Then suddenly one morning came a letter from Viola, and my heart seemed at the sight of it to fly upwards and forwards to the future as a swallow let out of a darkened room flies upwards and outwards with a swift rush to the open light.

"Bletchner's Hotel, Paris.
"If you wish, you may come to me."

That was all, but it was enough. Within a few moments I was ready for departure. For weeks a little case had stood ready packed against the wall of my room. All else was left standing.

I went to town, caught the morning train to Dover, and crossed to Calais.

I reached Paris finally about six and drove to a hotel. I dined in my travelling clothes in the restaurant, and then went up to my room to dress. What keen life I felt in all my veins! How strongly all the power of living had come back to me! Ordinarily, when we are well we get so accustomed to our health and strength we are hardly aware of either, but there are times when we become supremely conscious of both, as I was now. As I walked about my small apartment I felt a pride and joy in my strength such as a woman feels, I suppose, in her beauty when she surveys it in the mirror— a wild elation, a sense of triumph, as she realises in it her power. The thought of the approaching meeting with Viola danced before my mind, filling it with superb delight. All my veins seemed filled with fire instead of blood. My limbs and muscles flew to do the bidding of the eager, impatient brain.

I drove to Bletchner's Hotel and enquired for Madame Lonsdale, and was immediately shewn up to her suite of apartments. The salon I entered was empty. A door faced me at the other end. It was closed. My heart leapt up as I saw it. Was she there—just on the other side? The salon was lighted with shaded electric lamps and furnished and hung entirely in white, so that there was that dazzling effect of light I knew she always loved. I walked up and down in short quick turns, longing to go up to that tantalising door and knock, but holding myself back.

After a moment it opened and she came through it towards me. For one second before I rushed forward to clasp her in my arms, I stood to gaze at her, and the sweetness, the enchanting glamour of the vision was borne in upon me and locked itself into my memory for ever. She was in white, some soft white tissue that fell round her closely, edged with silver that seemed like moonlight on white clouds, and there was a little silver on her shoulders and round the breast that seemed like moonlight upon snow. Her fair hair shone in the blaze of light, her face raised to mine was pale and smiling, with a wonderful lustre in the azure eyes.

She seemed, as ever, the dream, the vision, the ideal, the unattainable divinity man's soul continually strives after.

A moment more and she was in my arms. Her physical semblance was mine, in which her spirit walked and moved, and I was the owner and conqueror of that at least.

"Trevor dear, be gentle!" she murmured in laughing remonstrance, but her white arms did not unlock from my neck nor her soft lips move far from mine.

"How happy I am now," she said, sinking into my embrace, "and how well you look, Trevor, how splendid! So strong and gloriously full of life!"

"I wonder I do," I answered, "after this cruel year you gave me. How could you leave me as you did while I was asleep beside you, and what was your reason? You will have to tell me now."

"I believe you would be happier if I did not, if you just trusted me and never asked to know," she answered, smiling back at me. "Are we not perfectly happy now? You have me again; look at me, am I just the same as when we parted?"

I looked at her intently, eagerly, my eyes drinking in all the perfect vision before me, each slim outline of the body, lying back now on the couch where we both were sitting, all the delicacy of the transparent skin, the smooth white forehead with its fine, straight-drawn eyebrows, the lovely eyes searching mine. Yes, I had lost nothing of my possession, and there seemed rather something added to that inner light and that wonderful look of intellect and power that shone through the face.

"I think you are the same," I said slowly, seeking vainly to express that indefinable extra light that seemed upon her face.

"Only perhaps more lovely. But tell me what your

reason was. I cannot bear to think there is a dark gap between us."

"You are so happy at this moment it seems a pity," she murmured softly. "You will not feel so happy when you know, and it's all over and past and forgotten. It's a thunderstorm that has rolled by and left us again in the sunlight. We are in Paradise now, are we not?"

I looked at her, and the triumph of delighted joy I had in her rose up to my brain, filling it, making all else seem obscure and of no account. Yet something in her words stirred my brain anxiously. Why should I mind hearing what she had to say? Was it possible that she had acted on her first letter to me, after all, and, while forcing freedom on me, taken it also for herself? Was it possible she had lent my possession, herself, to another? That blind, insensate jealousy of the male in physical matters instantly flamed up through me. In that moment of extreme passion for her, of expected triumph and delight, it burnt at its most furious pitch. I felt I must *know*, must drag the secret out of her, and if it was what I thought in that unreasoning moment, I would kill us both.

I threw myself forward on her so that she could not move. "Now tell me," I said. "You shall tell me, you promised you would."

Viola looked up at me with a regretful gaze but without any shrinking from my savage look and grasp.

"Certainly I will," she said gently; "but you will regret forcing me to tell you. Well, I left you, Trevor, because I found I was going to be the mother of your child."

"Viola!"

Had she stabbed me in the breast as I leant over her, the shock could not have been more great. To me the words seemed to go straight to my heart and stop it. I could not speak beyond that one word. For the moment I was absolutely stunned, paralysed. I took my hands from her arms which I had been holding, rose from the couch mechanically, and walked away from her, trying to realise, to understand what she had said and its meaning.

This was the fact that stood out most clearly before my disordered mental vision: knowing she was going to be in danger, to suffer, she had fled from me to bear the burden of it alone. And, next, that I had brought that burden and suffering on her. That spirit, so far above earthly things, as I always thought her, I had dragged down to know the common trials, share the common lot of earthly womanhood. The pain of these two ideas, the agony they brought with them to me in those moments was something almost unendurable. I felt crushed, absolutely ground into the dust before it. I sat down by the table and put both hands across my eyes, shutting out her exquisite vision, trying to shut out my thoughts. I felt as a religious enthusiast might feel who in a moment of drunken madness had outraged a sacred shrine.

Viola was to me, had always been, far more than a wife or a mistress is to a man; she was also the Idea to my brain, and what his Idea is to an artist an artist alone can know. But it is something he will live and die for, and count his heart's blood as nothing beside it. That she was a sacred thing, to be protected and guarded from the sordid incidents of daily life that she hated, had always been my thought. She was an artist, and as such had Art's own penalties to pay— the excessive nervous strain it puts upon the body, the long weakening tension, the extreme mental and bodily fatigue that sometimes accompanies or follows an artist's flight into the Elysian fields, from which he brings back those deathless flowers of music, verse, song, or colour to plant in the world. It is not fair that such a one should have to bear the common ills of life as well as pay those penalties.

That had always been my view. Viola was apart from the world, a daughter of the gods, not suited for, nor designed for the common sufferings of the clay. Love she might know, or rather must know, for love is always the handmaiden to Art, but motherhood, no. For those thousands and thousands of women who inhabit this world and have no divine gifts to bestow ma-

ternity is a pleasing and natural occupation; for the one amongst those thousands who has heard the Divine whisper and walked and conversed with the gods, and who can repeat those whispers to mortals, it is a waste of divine energy—a sacrilege. For genius is not handed down. It is given to one alone. It is not hereditary. For genius accumulated through heredity would at last produce a god. And that the jealous gods will not allow. Therefore the child of a genius is rarely a genius itself. It is born with a veil across its eyes that it may not see divinity and so return to the common type.

Knowing all this and feeling it keenly to my heart's core, I had given my promise to Viola. A promise, which indeed was part of a religion to me, and this was how I had kept it!

The intense humiliation of it all rolled through me, stunning me like a physical agony.

I heard her voice speaking gently to me, but I could not understand what she said, could not respond.

In memory, I was listening again to her voice when she had come that first night to the studio:

"You will not let our love drag us down to earth, will you? Let it only inspire us more. We will go to the Elysian fields together to gather the amaranth flowers. You will not try to turn me into the ordinary married woman. I could not accept those duties and that life. I want to live in my music, in the heaven of Ideas, as I do now. And to you I want always to be the vision, the dream, the spirit of your thoughts: never the wife, the mother, the keeper of the household, occupied with worldly matters."

And I had promised with all the rapture and the fervour of one who understood and thought her thoughts, and who had always longed to escape from the commonplace, the trivial matters of the world, to whom, as to her, the deathless amaranth flowers of beauty, of art, of Idea, of inspiration were all.

But the promise had been broken. Through me she had known pain, suffering, danger, inability to work, anxiety, daily care for months and months alone. The exquisite, perfect form I had counted so sacred, had suffered the common earthly lot. And through me. My thoughts seemed crushing me, grinding me beneath them, but at last her voice penetrated to my brain, through its anguish of self-reproach.

"I knew you would feel it so much, dear Trevor, that was why I kept it secret from you and went away, but now it is all over and past, you must not dwell on it. It is irrevocable. Don't reproach yourself about it. Let us be glad we are in Heaven now."

I rose and went over to her and knelt by the couch, raising one of her hands to my lips and holding it against me.

344

"Dear! Dearest one! You went away to endure all that misery alone, so that it should not distress me? How wonderfully unselfish you have always been to me!"

"Oh, no," she answered quickly, a light colour rising all over her face.

"You must not think that. I went away for myself, too. I could not bear that you should see me disfigured, spoiled, as you would think. I had always been the ideal to you. I could not bear to let you see me as an ordinary woman. I was afraid I should lose your passion for me, which I value more than anything else in the world. I felt I could face everything but that. Terrifying and horrible as it all was to meet quite alone, still it was better than feeling I was losing your love and desire."

"But you would not have done," I said vehemently; "nothing could make any difference to my love for you."

"Not to your love, perhaps, but our passions are not in our own control. They rise under certain influences, sink and decline under others, and we can do nothing. We must look these things in the face. See now, if I were suddenly turned to an old, old woman, withered before your eyes, would you feel as you feel now?"

"No," I answered slowly, "I admit old age . . ."

"Or hopelessly disfigured—my face rendered hideous by burns or loathsome with disease? You could not desire me then, I should not expect it. Love is unchangeable, but passion is a flame that shivers in every transient breeze. We can't help it. It *is* so. As I look at you now I love you for your strength and grace, above all for your beautiful form. If you hobbled into the room, bent and lame, I should love you still but not as I do now, quite, quite otherwise. And I was disfigured, temporarily, I know, but it went on for months and months. I was no longer your gay, glad spirit with the radiant wings. I was broken, distorted, hideous."

"Don't tell me," I muttered; "I can't bear it."

She put one arm round my neck and her soft lips on my hair.

"It is over," she whispered. "Do not be sorry, do not reproach yourself. It was so much better for you not to know, not to see it. It would all have preyed upon you so from day to day. *I* felt the long waiting. It seemed the time would never pass, and each day and night I felt so glad to know you were not there, to suffer with me, but away, quite out of reach of it all."

"But suppose you had died . . . without me."

"The chances were against that. And if I had, it would have still been better that you should be

346

away . . . for you. I would have come to you after death, really a spirit then, and lived ever after in your soul."

I put my arms round her, living, warm, beautiful, in the flesh.

"What a lonely, terrible year for you!" I said. "It never occurred to me . . . I never dreamed . . . and I can't understand now . . ."

"You remember the night I came back from Lawton's place to you? . . . You were mad with jealous rage, and I am so little accustomed to resist you . . . Well, it was my punishment for even thinking I could leave you . . . At least, I have always accepted it as such."

"I can never, never forgive myself."

"I knew you would take it like that, and now you see I can make you soon forget it. If you had felt like this for weeks and months it would almost have killed you."

She played with my hair and her lips touched my eyebrows.

"Where is the child?" I asked suddenly. "Did it die?"

"Yes," she answered, looking back at me sadly and closely. "Are you sorry?"

"No, I am not sorry," I answered savagely.

"I thought you would not be."

347

"Are you?"

She sighed.

"I hardly know. It was so like you, Trevor, such a very, very beautiful boy, exactly like you in miniature. I loved it, of course; I could not help it, but it is better as it is, better that it should die. We could not foresee how it would grow up, and so many men, the majority, are such monsters, such cruel fiends, it is really a crime to bring one into the world."

I was silent, thinking over that wonderful devotion and courage she had shewn me. Of all the solutions to the problem of her flight from me, this had never presented itself to my mind. We are taught both by tradition and experience how most women cling to their lover at such a time. Though indifferent, even faithless to him in their beauty and health, they come to him then for protection, for assistance. For their name's sake, to save their conventional honour, they will even accept marriage with one they no longer love, or force themselves on one they know has no longer love for them.

But how different this one, as always, had been! To preserve inviolate the spirit of our love, she had gone forward to meet what must to a sensitive nature like hers have been a time of horror and terror, absolutely alone, unsupported except by the thought that I was away, free, unable to share her misery!

With gifts in both hands she had come to me and laid them all in mine. Then, when I had broken my trust and brought distress upon her, when she was in need and I could have been the one to give, she had fled away from love, from consolation, from any return or reparation. Proud, courageous, independent, untamable, as she had always been, she was in comparison with other women as a lioness is to a gazelle.

I folded my arms round her tighter at these thoughts, for the lioness was mine and I owned her.

Perhaps, after all, it was worth while to suffer that agony of self-reproach I had just now, and was suffering still, to see put in such shining light before me her courage and her worth.

This was a white night, surely, as the others had been coloured, for as white is the blending of all the colours into one, so in this night all the emotions of those previous nights were blended. Passion, jealousy, triumph, and an agony like death had all swept over me in these few short hours, and now from them all, blent together and burning as metals in a smelter, rose up the extreme white vivid flame of love for her like the white silken tongue of fire, the last degree of fiercest heat that the smelter can produce.

I bent over her, looking down into her eyes, deep down into those living depths where I seemed to see the rays of an eternal heaven, clasping the smooth breast to me, closely, that its passionate heart-beats might answer my own, and in our veins burnt that intense white flame that melts into itself the glory of the immortal Spirit, the wonder of the hereafter, and all the joys of the world.

www.ingramcontent.com/pod-product-compliance
Lightning Source LLC
Chambersburg PA
CBHW080150060326
40689CB00018B/3928